Mohok
can
The higs Land
Gosen
ORANGE COM.
Courtland
Unter-Was ser gezet Land
Terra inundata.
WEST
CHESTER
Newtonn
Fairfield
Coffing
Haverstran
Orange
Norwalk P.
Pomton
BERGEN
COMIT.
Stanford
Patricks Ins.

MORIES
MORRIS COM.
Rockawway
Passaik Fl.
Hackinsak.
KentYork
Hammonek
Heu Rochel
Forse Neck
Block I.
Perecapanu
Hackinsak
Smith
Hutting
ton
Suffork Com.
Montagu P.
Wippany
Bergen
Oysterbau
Changewater
Veumark
Brockland
Float
Land
Jamaca
Union
ESSEY
QUEENS C.
RichmonaC.
KINGS COM.
Beach Littus
Woodbridge
Elisabeth
Town
Rawock
SANDSPITZE

Raroeton
Somerset
Braunschweig
Schrewsbury R.
Kings
town
SOMERSET
Laurandes
Heath
MIDDLESEX
Middleton
Longbridge
Shark R.
Trenton
Allens
town
Croswicks
Tinton
Schrewsbari
Squam R.
Burdenstown
MAPletkunck Riu.
Longinacoats
Goose
Cr.
Burlington
Mounthalli
Sheron
Ongs Cedar.
Islands Gift
Moor
field
Aurs
town
Ferekes Ra.
BURLINGTON COM.
Bellybrigde
Reads Muhl
Oyster
Creek
Barnegat
Eingang
CESTER
MIT.
Bury
muhl
Petits
Boden unfruchtbar
reuosa
vilis
Klein Eyhafen
Mihannan
Sandbanck
Morast
Paludes
Brigt Eingang
Brigt Gestad
Absecon Gestad
Gros Eyhafen
Pecks Gestad
Castonis Eingang
Ludleys Gestad
Louisends Eing.
Meilen Gestad
Herdfort Eingang
Turtle Gut
Kalte Quell
fons frigidus
May
Cape May
Com.
Ins.

NOVA VIRGINIANUM

MARE VIRGINIANUM

verfals
en

Legend

✳ METROPOLIS.
⊞ Urbs.
✣ Locus munitus.
○ Pagi.
△ Pagi Iuliei.
Town. Eine Stadt.
Savages, die Wilden.
Beach, Gestad.
Branch, Arm eines Flusses.
Cr. Creek, Ort zum anländern
Freshes W. Frisch Wasser.
Ridge, eine Reihe Hügel.
Riviera, Fluß.
Hill, Hügel.
Littus, Gestad.

Milliaria Germanica. 15. in uno Gradu.
5   10   15   20

Milliaria Anglica, quorů 60. in uno Gradu.
10   20   30   40

THE JOHN HARVARD LIBRARY

Howard Mumford Jones

Editor-in-Chief

JOURNEY TO PENNSYLVANIA

By

GOTTLIEB MITTELBERGER

Edited and Translated by
Oscar Handlin and John Clive

THE BELKNAP PRESS OF
HARVARD UNIVERSITY PRESS
Cambridge, Massachusetts
1 9 6 0

Distributed in Great Britain by Oxford University Press, London

Library of Congress Catalog Card Number 60-11555

Printed in the United States of America

CONTENTS

EDITORS' INTRODUCTION

WHEN William Penn received the charter for his province in America in 1681, he already had in mind the possibility that the territory granted him would become a refuge for the oppressed and the homeless people of the Old World. Humanitarian sentiment and reasonable calculation alike encouraged him in that expectation. Penn's sympathetic spirit imbued him with the desire to aid the unfortunate; and he knew that such settlers would make desirable colonists who would immensely increase the value of his property.

Penn had in mind, first of all, the needs of his fellow members in the Society of Friends. Still a despised and persecuted minority, these people had suffered much for their religion's sake and the proprietor was resolved to make Pennsylvania a place of safety for them in the wilderness. But Penn also gave some thought to the needs of the downtrodden Protestant sectarians of Germany. In his travels on the continent, he had caught a glimpse of their desperate situation, and he had perceived the utility of attracting some of them to the New World. His early pamphlet describing the opportunities of the province was quickly translated into German and seemed to welcome to America all who wished to come.[1]

Southwest Germany had indeed suffered cruelly in the

---

[1] C. M. Andrews, *Colonial Period of American History* (New Haven, 1937), III, 268 ff., 289 ff.

century before Pennsylvania was established; it was to continue to suffer for another century more. In Penn's day, distress was endemic in the area that stretched east of the Rhine north from Switzerland to the junction with the Main. Here were a multitude of little states, the greatest of which were the Duchies of Baden and Württemberg. Contiguous to them was the Palatinate lying on both sides of the Rhine beyond the point where it bent westward to the sea.

These unstable lands had long tempted the avarice and ambition of neighboring rulers who, for decades, had fought across them. Religious wars, the aftermath of the Reformation, had added other sources of dissension. A good part of the Thirty Years' War had been fought across this territory; and although that conflict had ended in 1648, peace did not come. Dynastic wars succeeded one another in wearisome monotony on through the seventeenth and into the eighteenth centuries.

Pervasive poverty was the product of these disorders. Even in normal times agriculture was depressed; and the situation was frequently made worse by famines and crop failures. A host of wretched peasants lived always at the very margin of existence.

Perhaps as a result of the misery of their lot in this world, the peasants and artisans of the Rhineland were subject to recurrent religious revivals. A multitude of mystical sects flourished in the area, holding forth to true believers the promise of future redemption as compensation for the trials of the present. Often, alas, their enthusiasm and disregard for the rules of the established church of the government brought them into conflict with the authorities and increased the difficulties of their adherents.

In a region so given to disorder numerous families were ready to heed the call to migration. Great masses of men, in desperation, grasped at the belief that any alternative was preferable to the misery in which they were engulfed. Some of the peasants from the Rhineland began to move eastward to Hungary and later to Rumania and Russia. Others turned their eyes westward where the wonders of a New World seemed to await them. These men would be particularly sensitive to William Penn's appeal.[2]

In 1683 Francis Daniel Pastorius led the first band of families from the Rhine Valley to Philadelphia, on the outskirts of which he established the settlement of Germantown. This was a fortunate group, blessed with able leadership and composed of resourceful, hard-working men. It prospered at once. The news of this thriving community spread through Germany in the next half century and attracted thousands of Pastorius' countrymen to the New World. A large number of them continued to come to Pennsylvania, spreading from Philadelphia to the neighboring counties in ever growing settlements.[3]

Relatively few residents of the Rhineland, however, had the financial resources adequate to meet the needs of settlement in America as Pastorius had. Yet, it was precisely among the poorest folk, among those with the least resources, that the fever to make a new start across the ocean burned most intensely. If they were to go at all it would only be with some external assistance.

---

[2] On the German background *see* Albert B. Faust, *German Element in the United States* (New York, 1927), I, 53 ff.; Karl Weller, *Württembergische Geschichte* (Stuttgart, 1957), pp. 119 ff.

[3] Theodore W. Bean, ed., *History of Montgomery County, Pennsylvania* (Philadelphia, 1884), pp. 133 ff.

By the end of the seventeenth century, the American colonies had developed a system that enabled would-be migrants from England to finance the cost of their voyage out of the proceeds of their future labor. This system rested upon the legally binding force of a contract by which an individual sold his services for a specified term. The planters and farmers of the New World, eager for labor, which was always in short supply, willingly paid the price of transportation, while the poor peasants and servants, eager to migrate, willingly signed the indentures that disposed of their services for a term. Such arrangements were the basis for a thriving trade in indentured servants. Men who wished to make the crossing found ship captains and merchants willing to advance them the cost of the journey on these terms. The American landowners paid the price in return for the hands they needed. And these merchants and captains profited as intermediaries.[4]

The practice spread to Germany in the eighteenth century. The costs and the risks were, of course, greater for emigrants who came from the continent than for those from England. But an ingenious modification in the system guaranteed that the whole burden of the added cost and added risk would fall upon the immigrants themselves. The German passenger who set out for America did not have a contract or indenture as his English counterpart did, in which were detailed the exact conditions of his future service. Rather, the German embarked after having made only a verbal agreement on the price of his passage, to be paid after

---

[4] *See* A. E. Smith, *Colonists in Bondage* (Chapel Hill, 1947); C. A. Herrick, *White Servitude in Pennsylvania* (Philadelphia, 1926); Paul Kapff, "Schwaben in Amerika," *Württembergische Neujahrsblätter*, X (1893), 17 ff.

arrival in America by his future master. In the New World, his labor would be auctioned off to whoever would pay the cost of his redemption. Such Redemptioners were therefore entirely helpless in fixing the terms of their service. They were, as a result, subject to merciless exploitation as Mittelberger pointed out.[5]

However harsh these conditions were, they did not dim the attractions of the golden land. In the stories that drifted back to Germany, the splendors of the New World glistened by contrast with the miseries of the Old. And all those who profited by the trade had an interest in magnifying the impression that the opportunities America offered were limitless. The agents of the ship captains, the Newlanders whom Mittelberger described with such distaste, spread fabulous accounts of the wealth available for the taking and kept the immigration fever at a peak.[6]

As a result, the volume of migration rose rapidly, reaching a high point between 1749 and 1754 when more than 30,000 Germans came to Pennsylvania. The number of Germans in the Province grew steadily through the first half of the eighteenth century. Although Mittelberger may have been misled in his estimates, by 1750 his countrymen probably formed one-third of the population of the colony.[7]

The Germans were strangers in the New World, as all Europeans were, cut off from the familiar landscape and

[5] See Christopher Saur's letter to Governor Morris, March 15, 1755, quoted in Frank R. Diffenderffer, *The German Immigration into Pennsylvania, Part II The Redemptioners* (Lancaster, 1900), pp. 241 ff.; also Bean, *Montgomery County*, pp. 297 ff.

[6] For the Newlanders, *see also* Oscar Kuhns, *The German and Swiss Settlements of Colonial Pennsylvania* (New York, 1901), pp. 77 ff.

[7] Kuhns, *German and Swiss Settlements*, p. 57; Herrick, *White Servitude*, pp. 168 ff.

activities of home. But in addition, the newcomers from the Rhineland found themselves foreigners to those among whom they lived not only in language but also in religion. For those among the Germans who belonged to one or another of the numerous dissident sects, this was an opportunity. America was the empty space in which they could enact their own peculiar experiments in holy living. The members of the Reformed Church also adjusted to conditions in the New World with relatively little difficulty. But the adherents of the established Lutheran Church faced the greatest problems. In coming to Pennsylvania, they had lost the support of the State; and they found it necessary to reconstruct the churches they had known at home by their own efforts.

This problem was a source of concern to all German immigrants, including the residents of The Trappe, a village in Upper Providence Township, some eight miles from Norristown and halfway between Philadelphia and Reading.

The Trappe had originally been part of the Proprietor's Manor of Gilberts but the land had gradually been alienated by the Penns and in the early eighteenth century began to receive a mounting stream of settlers, many of them Germans. In 1717, for instance, Jacob Schrack brought his family from Germantown to lay out a farm of two hundred and fifty acres. Others of his compatriots joined him and soon a village appeared complete with shop and tavern. Among these newcomers were the adherents of many sects, but the Lutherans were probably the most numerous.[8]

The members of the Reformed Church and the sectarians

[8] W. J. Buck, *History of Montgomery County* (Norristown, 1859), pp. 102 ff.; Bean, *Montgomery County*, pp. 366 ff.; C. R. Barker, "Lost Townships of Montgomery County," Historical Society of Montgomery County, *Bulletin*, I (1938), pp. 207 ff.

quickly organized their own congregations, but the Lutherans were slower to do so. That was why Schrack, among others, felt the need for some provision for Lutheran religious worship. He seems early to have been in correspondence with the ecclesiastical authorities in London and Halle requesting assistance. Such appeals at last evoked a response from the Reverend Henry Melchior Muhlenberg, a young clergyman imbued with missionary zeal.

Muhlenberg had been born in 1711, the son of a shoemaker. He had studied at Göttingen and Jena and had served as pastor in an orphanage when, in 1741, at the age of thirty he assumed the charge of the parishes in Upper (then, New) Providence, Philadelphia, and New Hanover. He arrived in New Providence in November 1742 to find there a congregation of fifty members worshipping in a barn. He quickly began to reorganize the life of the community. An appropriate church building was started in 1743 and finished two years later.[9]

The building was a substantial structure that would remain in service for fully a century. But it lacked an organ. To supply that want, Muhlenberg arranged to purchase instruments in Germany for shipment to his congregations in America. At the arrival of the organs Muhlenberg presided over their consecration with great pleasure. But as a byproduct, their importation afforded Gottlieb Mittelberger the opportunity to come to the New World.[10]

Of Mittelberger's early life we know little. He was a native of Enzweihingen, a small town near Vaihingen in the Duchy

[9] Clifton S. Hunsicker, *Montgomery County Pennsylvania a History* (New York, 1923), pp. 122 ff., 128, 129, 328 ff.

[10] Henry M. Muhlenberg, *Journals* (Philadelphia, 1942), I, 276.

of Württemberg. The district had suffered greatly during
the wars of the preceding century. Mittelberger evidently
had enough education to serve as a teacher and to be able
to write a literate account of his journeys. Yet he did not con-
sider himself an educated man and the style of his work,
replete with provincialisms, showed that he was not a university graduate. Certainly he would somewhere have mentioned any such distinction had he enjoyed it; and sig-
nificantly Muhlenberg's journals contain not a reference to
him.

Mittelberger was an earnest, dedicated man who had ap-
parently accepted the invitation to come to America without a clear consciousness of what was involved in the journey or in the process of settlement. Consequently he was
often to be surprised by the rude life he found across the
ocean.

Mittelberger arrived in Philadelphia late in 1750, one of
almost five hundred passengers on the ship *Osgood*, Captain
William Wilkie commanding. On September 29 at the courthouse Mittelberger took the necessary oath of allegiance.
He was then free to settle in New Providence as organist
and schoolmaster. He was unhappy at the crudity of the
society about him; and he missed the wife and children he
had left at home. Very likely he was also dissatisfied with the
low salary accorded him and had some quarrels with his
neighbors. In 1754 after somewhat less than four years of
residence he returned to his native place. There he seems
to have settled down and to have spent his remaining days
in obscurity. He had no further contact with America. Ap-
propriately, two generations later, when the cooper, Christian Mittelberger — who may have been Gottlieb's grand-

son — emigrated from Enzweihingen, it was eastward to Russia.[11]

Gottlieb Mittelberger brought back with him an admiration of some aspects of the life of the country in which he had passed this brief period. But he was also shocked, as many Europeans were, by the consequences of relative freedom from traditional restraints in the colonies. Mittelberger was distressed by the disregard for rank, by the religious laxity, and the easy manners of the back-country Pennsylvanians. Above all he was tormented by fearsome memories of the miseries that his fellow countrymen had encountered on the way to the New World and in the first years of their adjustment. And he was determined to expose the frauds of the Newlanders who misled so many Germans by their fanciful accounts of conditions in America. His book was to set the record straight.

In 1756, his printed account appeared as a small volume of 120 pages. He seems to have had the aid of an unknown editor, one somewhat more learned than himself, who supplied the references to other works and corrected the spelling, but left the grammar and construction untouched. The first edition was published in Frankfurt and Leipzig; another was issued during the same year in Stuttgart. This was his only published work.[12]

[11] Ralph Beaver Strassburger, *Pennsylvania German Pioneers* (Norristown, 1934), I, 414–415; Bean, *Montgomery County*, p. 1064; Friedrich Wissmann, *Die Heimat. Kreis Vaihingen-Enz* (Bietigheim, 1954), pp. 13, 99–109; C. Belschner, *Geschichte von Württemberg* (Stuttgart, 1902), p. 403; *Beschreibung des Königreichs Württemberg* (Stuttgart, 1856), XXXVI, 131 ff.; Charles L. Maurer, "Early Lutheran Education in Pennsylvania," Pennsylvania German Society, *Proceedings*, XL (1929), 116; Karl Stumpp, *Ostwanderung. Akten über die Auswanderung der Württemberger nach Russland 1816–1822* (Leipzig, 1941), p. 156.

[12] See Joseph Sabin, *Bibliotheca Americana* (New York, 1880), XII, No. 49761; Karper's *Bücherlexicon* (Leipzig, 1835), Vols. III, IV.

Mittelberger's narrative was written in a simple but lively style. He himself warns the reader not to expect too rigid an organization of the book. His method of telling about his observations and adventures could almost be called stream-of-consciousness. He is led from one subject to another by associations that come to his mind. This weakens the structure of the account, but adds to its charm. Statistics, geographical information, comments on institutions, anecdotes, and personal experiences follow each other helter-skelter. But the author's shrewd common sense, his powers of observation, his ingenious humor, his curiosity, and his genuine love of nature combine to lend a unique and attractive character to the story of his travels.

Mittelberger's language was the uncultivated Swabian dialect of Württemberg, heavily charged with colloquialisms. The work seems on the whole accurate in its narration of the author's direct observations. Mittelberger, however, showed the European's usual gullibility when it came to repeating second-hand accounts of what certain Indians had seen or done and of the peculiarities of nature in America.

The portrayal of the conditions of immigration and of the lot of the Redemptioners is highly charged with emotion; Mittelberger, after all, was a passenger on one of these ships. But his descriptions are neither overdrawn nor unfair. Later scholars who have reviewed the evidence have been well impressed by the accuracy of the book. In its own day it appears to have been widely read and extensively quoted. But it did not halt the flow to America of Redemptioners who continued to be attracted by the opportunities Mittelberger did not perceive.[13]

[13] Faust, *German Element,* I, 61, 70, II, 381; C. F. Huch, "Mittelbergers

It did however add fuel to the developing controversy over the character of the New World. Writers in the latter half of the eighteenth century borrowed freely from it, as they did from Peter Kalm's journals, as they pursued the intellectually intriguing argument over whether American conditions could or could not produce a civilization.[14]

The book remained well known in the nineteenth century and occasional passages from it were rendered into English from time to time. But a full-scale translation did not appear until the very end of the century. At that time, a growing interest among the descendants of the Pennsylvania Germans in their own history had led to the establishment of the Pennsylvania German Society. Prominent Pennsylvanians encouraged research in the history of the eighteenth century, and such research emphasized the importance of Mittelberger's account.[15]

Such interest encouraged Charles (or Karl) Theodore Eben to undertake a translation. Eben had been born in 1836 and came to Philadelphia in 1863. His father was a hatter and he himself eked out a livelihood as a professor of

---

Reise nach Pennsylvanien," *Mitteilungen des Deutschen Pionier-Vereins von Philadelphia*, XXII (1911), 29 ff.; M. D. Learned, "Gottlieb Mittelbergers Reise nach Pennsylvanien und ihre Bedeutung als Kulturbild," Society for the History of the Germans in Maryland, *Fifth Annual Report* (1890–1891), pp. 23 ff.

[14] *See*, for example, [Cornelius van Pauw] *Recherches philosophiques sur les Américains* (Berlin, 1768; reprinted London, 1771); [Corneilius de Pauw] *Défense des recherches philosophiques sur les Américains* (Berlin, 1770); [Ant. Jos. Pernety] *Examen des recherches philosophiques sur l'Amérique* (Berlin, 1771). Mittelberger and Kalm were also the sources of [Jacques Philibert Rousselot de Surgy] *Histoire naturelle et politique de la Pennsylvanie . . .* Tr. de l'allemand (Paris, 1768). *See also* E. E. Doll, *American History as Interpreted by German Historians* (Philadelphia, 1949), pp. 464, 481.

[15] For the earlier translation by Henry S. Dotterer, *see* Bean, *Montgomery County*, p. 1064. *See also* Diffenderfer, *German Immigration*, pp. 177 ff.

languages. He wrote a German primer for Americans and an English primer for Germans, and also translated into German the works of Poe and other English and American authors.[16]

William E. Whitman, a well-known attorney, was among those who encouraged Eben to prepare an English edition of Mittelberger's account. The translation, published in Philadelphia in 1898, gave a general picture of the contents of the book, but was inadequate in its rendition of the eighteenth-century German and lost much of the tone of the original. It quickly went out of print.[17]

The present translation has been made directly from the original of the first German (Frankfurt) edition, a copy of which is in the Boston Athenaeum. The translation is, in general, a literal rendition of the original. However, the translators have felt justified in modernizing the spelling of place and personal names where the author was clearly ignorant or in error. Usually it seemed desirable to preserve the units Mittelberger used for measurements of currency and lands, with their equivalents supplied in eighteenth-century English terms only when necessary to make the meaning clear.

Several footnotes in the text of the original edition bear the appearance of additions by the first editor, intended to add

[16] For Eben, *see*: Philadelphia directories, 1859–1865; *A Comprehensive German Primer* (Brooklyn, 1882); *Eben's Sprachmeister* (New York, 1890). His translations from Poe, Lowell, and Tennyson appeared in 1864, and in 1865 he published a German version of Franklin Crosby's life of Lincoln.

[17] *Gottlieb Mittelberger's Journey to Pennsylvania in the Year 1750 and Return to Germany in the Year 1754, Containing Not Only a Description of the Country According to Its Present Condition, but also a Detailed Account of the Sad and Unfortunate Circumstances of Most of the Germans That Have Emigrated or Are Emigrating to that Country.* Translated from the German by Carl Theo. Eben, Member of the German Society of Pennsylvania (Philadelphia: John Jos. McVey, 1898).

learned references to the author's simple account. In most cases they stand as originally printed and are distinguished by asterisks. The editors have occasionally supplied explanatory footnotes of their own where the text seemed to demand them. These are indicated by numerical superscripts. Place names have been located with the aid of a contemporary German map.[18]

---

[18] *Pensylvania Nova Jersey et Nova York cum Regionibus ad Fluvium Delaware in America Sitis, Nova Delineatione ob Oculos Posita per Tob[ias] Conr[ad] Lotter Geographum.* Aug[ustae] Vind[elicorum]. C. 1750.

GOTTLIEB MITTELBERGER'S

JOURNEY

TO

PENNSYLVANIA

IN THE YEAR 1750

AND

RETURN TO GERMANY

IN THE YEAR 1754

Containing

not only a description of the country in its present condition, but also a detailed account of the sad and unfortunate circumstances of most of the Germans who have moved to that country or are about to do so.

To the Most Illustrious
Prince and Lord
Carl
Duke of Württemberg and Teck, Count of
Mömpelgard, Lord of Heidenheim and
Justingen, etc. Knight of the Golden
Fleece, and Field Marshal of the
Illustrious Swabian Circle etc.

To my most gracious Prince and Lord I dedicate in the most profound submission in its present revised form the humble publication parts of which Your Illustrious Princely Highness graciously deigned to peruse in manuscript, and I commend myself to a continuance of your high princely grace and favor.

Gottlieb Mittelberger

PREFACE TO THE FIRST EDITION

ESTEEMED READER

THE value of this little book does not lie in its elegant and elaborate composition, but in its remarkable contents. The former should not be expected from the author who is not a scholar. But his narrative, which, by the way, may be easily read, serves as testimony of his sincerity and, in addition, of the fact that he writes for the most part as an eyewitness. Inasmuch as he did not aim strictly to narrate all subjects of the same kind consecutively, his work has some variety — which is, perhaps, more agreeable to the reader. For the most part the author's artless and unornamented account of the habits of various Europeans and of the American savages, of their laws, their customs, their domestic and religious institutions, is new, and of such a nature that the reflective reader will be delighted to perceive in it a peculiar mixture of the European and the American environment, of the customs of the Old and the New World, and of a people living partly in civilization and partly in a state of natural freedom.

The information the book contains about the kingdom of nature — about animals, plants, etc. — should attract the attention of the reader no less, inasmuch as the wise Creator has in this land placed an entirely new arena to display his miracles before the eyes of rational men.

But the most important part of this publication undoubtedly lies in the account of the fate that awaits most of those unfortunate people who leave Germany in order to seek an uncertain fortune in the New World; and who find instead, if not death, surely oppressive servitude and slavery.

Nothing has been changed in the author's work, except that some notes taken from other writers of repute and confirming the author's narrative have been added to the text; and the spelling has been made to conform to that in general use. The little work is hereby warmly recommended to the reader.

[There follows a German translation of the English testimonial quoted below, page 8.]

I
THE CROSSING
TO PENNSYLVANIA

I

THE CROSSING
TO PENNSYLVANIA

In the month of May 1750 I left my birthplace Enzweihingen in the district of Vaihingen for Heilbronn, where an
organ was waiting for me, ready to be shipped to Pennsylvania. With this organ I took the usual route down the
Neckar and the Rhine to Rotterdam in Holland. From Rotterdam I sailed with a transport of approximately 400 souls
— Württemberger, Durlacher, Palatines, and Swiss, etc. —
across the North Sea to Cowes in England; and, after a
nine-day stopover there, across the Atlantic, until at last on
the tenth of October 1750 I landed in Philadelphia, the
capital of Pennsylvania.[1]

The trip from home to Rotterdam including the sojourn
there, took fully seven weeks because of the many delays
encountered both in going down the Rhine and in Holland.
Without these one could have completed the journey more
quickly. The voyage from Rotterdam to Philadelphia took
fifteen weeks. I spent nearly four years in America and, as
my testimonials show, held the post of organist and school-
teacher in the German St. Augustine's Church in Providence.
Besides that I gave private music and German lessons in the

[1] Mittelberger uses new style dating, which causes a discrepancy with
dates given elsewhere. *See below*, p. 93.

7

house of Captain von Diemer, as attested by the following certificate:

Whereas the bearer Mr. Mittelberger, music master, has resolved to return from this province to his native land, which is in the Duchy of Württemberg in Germany, I have at his request granted these lines to certify that the above named Mr. Mittelberger has behaved himself honestly, diligently, and faithfully in the offices of schoolmaster and organist during the space of three years in the Township of New-Providence, County of Philadelphia and Province of Pennsylvania, &c. So that I and all his employers were entirely satisfied, and would willingly have him to remain with us. But as his call obliges him to proceed on his long journey, we would recommend the said Mr. Mittelberger to all persons of dignity and character; and beg their assistance, so that he may pass and repass until he arrives at his respective abode; which may God grant, and may the benediction of Heaven accompany him in his journey. Deus benedicat susceptis ejus ferat eum ad amicos suos maxima prosperitate.[2]
Dabam, Providentiae Philadelphiae

 Comitatu Pennsylvania in America,
 die 25. Apr. A. D. 1754 [3]

     John Diemer, Cap.
     Sam. Kennedy, M.D.
     Henry Pawling, Esqr.

 T.[4]
Henry Marsteller
Matthias Gmelin.

I made careful inquiries into the conditions of the country. And what I am going to describe in this book I partly found out for myself, and partly heard from reliable people who know what they were talking about. I should no doubt have been able to report and to recount more if, at the time,

[2] May God bless his undertaking and bring him to his friends with the greatest dispatch.
[3] Given at Providence in the County of Philadelphia, Pennsylvania in America on April 25, 1754.
[4] Witnesses.

I had ever considered publishing anything about Pennsylvania. But I always thought myself far too feeble to do that sort of thing. It was only the misfortunes I encountered on my voyage to and fro (for in the country itself things went well with me, because I was able to earn a living right away, and could easily support myself well) and the nasty tricks the Newlanders wanted to play on me and my family, as I shall relate further on, that first gave me the idea not to keep what I knew to myself.

But what really drove me to write this little book was the sad and miserable condition of those traveling from Germany to the New World, and the irresponsible and merciless proceedings of the Dutch traders in human beings and their man-stealing emissaries — I mean the so-called Newlanders. For these at one and the same time steal German people under all sorts of fine pretexts, and deliver them into the hands of the great Dutch traffickers in human souls. From this business the latter make a huge profit, and the Newlanders a smaller one.

This, as I say, is the principal reason for my publishing this little book. In fact, I had to take a solemn oath to write it. For before I left Pennsylvania, when it became known that I wanted to return to Württemberg, numerous Württemberger, Durlacher, and Palatines (a great many of whom live there and spend their days moaning and groaning about ever having left their native country) begged me with tears and uplifted hands, and even in the name of God, to publicize their misery and sorrow in Germany. So that not only the common people but even princes and lords might be able to hear about what happened to them; and so that innocent souls would no longer leave their native country, persuaded to do so by the Newlanders, and dragged by them into a similar kind of slavery. And so I vowed to the great God, and promised those people to reveal the entire truth about it to people in Germany, according to the best of my knowledge and ability.

I hope, therefore, that my dear countrymen and indeed all of Germany will be no less concerned to get news and factual information about how far it is to Pennsylvania and how long it takes to get there; about what the journey costs, and what discomforts and dangers one has to undergo in the bargain; about what happens when the people arrive in America well or ill; about how they are sold and scattered around; and, finally, about what conditions in general are like. I conceal neither good nor bad aspects; and thus I hope that the world, liking an honest man, will look on me as impartial and truthful. Once people have read all this I have no doubt that those who might still have some desire to go over there will stay at home and will carefully avoid this long and difficult voyage and the misfortunes connected with it; since such a journey will mean for most who undertake it the loss of all they possess, of freedom and peace, and for some the loss of their very lives and, I can even go so far as to say, of the salvation of their souls.

To travel from Durlach or Württemberg as far as Holland and the open sea one must reckon on a trip of 200 hours.[5] From there across the sea to England as far as Cowes, where all ships drop anchor before they finally begin the great ocean crossing, another 150 hours. From there over 100 hours until one completely loses sight of England. Then across the At-

[5] Mittelberger, as was contemporary German practice, uses stunden or hours as a measure of distance, conventionally equal to 3.75 to 4 kilometers, or about 2.4 miles.

lantic, that is from land to land, as the sailors put it, 1,200 hours. Finally from the first sight of land in Pennsylvania to Philadelphia, over 40 hours. Altogether such a journey adds up to 1,700 hours or 1,700 French miles.

This journey lasts from the beginning of May until the end of October, that it, a whole six months, and involves such hardships that it is really impossible for any description to do justice to them. The reason for this is that the Rhine boats must pass by thirty-six different customs houses between Heilbronn and Holland. At each of these all the ships must be examined, and these examinations take place at the convenience of the customs officials. Meanwhile, the ships with the people in them are held up for a long time. This involves a great deal of expense for the passengers; and it also means that the trip down the Rhine alone takes from four to six weeks.

When the ships with their passengers arrive in Holland they are there held up once again for from five to six weeks. Because everything is very expensive in Holland the poor people must spend nearly all they own during this period. In addition various sad accidents are likely to occur here. I have, for instance, seen with my own eyes two of the children of a man trying to board ship near Rotterdam meet sudden death by drowning.

In Rotterdam, and to some extent also in Amsterdam, the people are packed into the big boats as closely as herring, so to speak. The bedstead of one person is hardly two feet across and six feet long, since many of the boats carry from four to six hundred passengers, not counting the immense amount of equipment, tools, provisions, barrels of fresh water, and other things that also occupy a great deal of space.

Because of contrary winds it sometimes takes the boats from two to four weeks to make the trip from Holland to Cowes. But, given favorable winds, that voyage can be completed in eight days or less. On arrival everything is examined once more and customs duties paid. It can happen that ships have to ride at anchor there from eight to fourteen days, or until they have taken on full cargoes. During this time everyone has to spend his last remaining money and to consume the provisions that he meant to save for the ocean voyage, so that most people must suffer tremendous hunger and want at sea where they really feel the greatest need. Many thus already begin their sufferings on the voyage between Holland and England.

When the ships have weighed anchor for the last time, usually off Cowes in Old England, then both the long sea voyage and misery begin in earnest. For from there the ships often take eight, nine, ten, or twelve weeks sailing to Philadelphia, if the wind is unfavorable. But even given the most favorable winds, the voyage takes seven weeks.

During the journey the ship is full of pitiful signs of distress — smells, fumes, horrors, vomiting, various kinds of sea sickness, fever, dysentery, headaches, heat, constipation, boils, scurvy, cancer, mouth-rot, and similar afflictions, all of them caused by the age and the highly-salted state of the food, especially of the meat, as well as by the very bad and filthy water, which brings about the miserable destruction and death of many. Add to all that shortage of food, hunger, thirst, frost, heat, dampness, fear, misery, vexation, and lamentation as well as other troubles. Thus, for example, there are so many lice, especially on the sick people, that they have to be scraped off the bodies. All this misery reaches

12

its climax when in addition to everything else one must also suffer through two to three days and nights of storm, with everyone convinced that the ship with all aboard is bound to sink. In such misery all the people on board pray and cry pitifully together.

In the course of such a storm the sea begins to surge and rage so that the waves often seem to rise up like high mountains, sometimes sweeping over the ship; and one thinks that he is going to sink along with the ship. All the while the ship, tossed by storm and waves, moves constantly from one side to the other, so that nobody aboard can either walk, sit, or lie down and the tightly packed people on their cots, the sick as well as the healthy, are thrown every which way. One can easily imagine that these hardships necessarily affect many people so severely that they cannot survive them.

I myself was afflicted by severe illness at sea, and know very well how I felt. These people in their misery are many times very much in want of solace, and I often entertained and comforted them with singing, praying, and encouragement. Also, when possible, and when wind and waves permitted it, I held daily prayer meetings with them on deck, and, since we had no ordained clergyman on board, was forced to administer baptism to five children. I also held services, including a sermon, every Sunday, and when the dead were buried at sea, commended them and our souls to the mercy of God.

Among those who are in good health impatience sometimes grows so great and bitter that one person begins to curse the other, or himself and the day of his birth, and people sometimes come close to murdering one another. Misery and malice are readily associated, so that people

13

begin to cheat and steal from one another. And then one always blames the other for having undertaken the voyage. Often the children cry out against their parents, husbands against wives and wives against husbands, brothers against their sisters, friends and acquaintances against one another.

But most of all they cry out against the thieves of human beings! Many groan and exclaim: "Oh! If only I were back at home, even lying in my pig-sty!" Or they call out: "Ah, dear God, if I only once again had a piece of good bread or a good fresh drop of water." Many people whimper, sigh, and cry out pitifully for home. Most of them become homesick at the thought that many hundreds of people must necessarily perish, die, and be thrown into the ocean in such misery. And this in turn makes their families, or those who were responsible for their undertaking the journey, oftentimes fall almost into despair — so that it soon becomes practically impossible to rouse them from their depression. In a word, groaning, crying, and lamentation go on aboard day and night; so that even the hearts of the most hardened, hearing all this, begin to bleed.

One can scarcely conceive what happens at sea to women in childbirth and to their innocent offspring. Very few escape with their lives; and mother and child, as soon as they have died, are thrown into the water. On board our ship, on a day on which we had a great storm, a woman about to give birth and unable to deliver under the circumstances, was pushed through one of the portholes into the sea because her corpse was far back in the stern and could not be brought forward to the deck.

Children between the ages of one and seven seldom survive the sea voyage; and parents must often watch their offspring suffer miserably, die, and be thrown into the ocean, from want, hunger, thirst, and the like. I myself, alas, saw such a pitiful fate overtake thirty-two children on board our vessel, all of whom were finally thrown into the sea. Their parents grieve all the more, since their children do not find repose in the earth, but are devoured by the predatory fish of the ocean. It is also worth noting that children who have not had either measles or smallpox usually get them on board the ship and for the most part perish as a result.

On one of these voyages a father often becomes infected by his wife and children, or a mother by her small children, or even both parents by their children, or sometimes whole families one by the other, so that many times numerous corpses lie on the cots next to those who are still alive, especially when contagious diseases rage on board.

Many other accidents also occur on these ships, especially falls in which people become totally crippled and can never be completely made whole again. Many also tumble into the sea.

It is not surprising that many passengers fall ill, because in addition to all the other troubles and miseries, warm food is served only three times a week, and at that is very bad, very small in quantity, and so dirty as to be hardly palatable at all. And the water distributed in these ships is often very black, thick with dirt, and full of worms. Even when very thirsty, one is almost unable to drink it without loathing. It is certainly true that at sea one would often spend a great deal of money just for one good piece of bread, or one good drink of water — not even to speak of a good glass of wine — if one could only obtain them. I have, alas, had to experience that myself. For toward the end of the voyage we had to eat

15

the ship's biscuit, which had already been spoiled for a long time, even though in no single piece was there more than the size of a thaler that was not full of red worms and spiders' nests. True, great hunger and thirst teach one to eat and drink everything — but many must forfeit their lives in the process. It is impossible to drink sea water, since it is salty and bitter as gall. If this were not the case, one could undertake such an ocean voyage with far less expense and without so many hardships.

When at last after the long and difficult voyage the ships finally approach land, when one gets to see the headlands for the sight of which the people on board had longed so passionately, then everyone crawls from below to the deck, in order to look at the land from afar. And people cry for joy, pray, and sing praises and thanks to God. The glimpse of land revives the passengers, especially those who are half-dead of illness. Their spirits, however weak they had become, leap up, triumph, and rejoice within them. Such people are now willing to bear all ills patiently, if only they can disembark soon and step on land. But, alas, alas!

When the ships finally arrive in Philadelphia after the long voyage only those are let off who can pay their sea freight or can give good security. The others, who lack the money to pay, have to remain on board until they are purchased and until their purchasers can thus pry them loose from the ship. In this whole process the sick are the worst off, for the healthy are preferred and are more readily paid for. The miserable people who are ill must often still remain at sea and in sight of the city for another two or three weeks — which in many cases means death. Yet many of them, were they able to pay their debts and to leave the ships at once, might escape with their lives.

Before I begin to describe how this commerce in human beings takes place I must report what the voyage to Philadelphia or Pennsylvania costs. Any one older than ten years has to pay £10, or 60 florins, for the passage from Rotterdam to Philadelphia. Children between five and ten pay half fare, that is to say £5, or 30 florins. All children under the age of five get free passage. In return the passengers are transported across the ocean; and as long as they are at sea, they get their board, however bad it is (as I reported above).

All this covers only the sea voyage; the cost of land transportation from home to Rotterdam, including the Rhine passage, comes to at least 40 florins no matter how economically one tries to live on the way. This does not include the expenses of any extraordinary contingencies. I can assure readers of this much — that many travelers on the journey from their homes to Philadelphia spent 200 florins, even with all possible thrift.

This is how the commerce in human beings on board ship takes place. Every day Englishmen, Dutchmen, and High Germans come from Philadelphia and other places, some of them very far away, sometime twenty or thirty or forty hours' journey, and go on board the newly arrived vessel that has brought people from Europe and offers them for sale. From among the healthy they pick out those suitable for the purposes for which they require them. Then they negotiate with them as to the length of the period for which they will go into service in order to pay off their passage, the whole amount of which they generally still owe. When an agreement has been reached, adult persons by written contract bind themselves to serve for three, four, five, or six years, according to their health and age. The very young, between the ages of ten and fifteen, have to serve until they are twenty-one, however.

Many parents in order to pay their fares in this way and get off the ship must barter and sell their children as if they were cattle. Since the fathers and mothers often do not know where or to what masters their children are to be sent, it frequently happens that after leaving the vessel, parents and children do not see each other for years on end, or even for the rest of their lives.

People who arrive without the funds to pay their way and who have children under the age of five, cannot settle their debts by selling them. They must give away these children for nothing to be brought up by strangers; and in return these children must stay in service until they are twenty-one years old. Children between five and ten who owe half-fare, that is, thirty florins, must also go into service in return until they are twenty-one years old, and can neither set free their parents nor take their debts upon themselves. On the other hand, the sale of children older than ten can help to settle a part of their parents' passage charges.

A wife must be responsible for her sick husband and a husband for his sick wife, and pay his or her fare respectively, and must thus serve five to six years not only for herself or himself, but also for the spouse, as the case may be. If both should be ill on arrival, then such persons are brought directly from the ship into a hospital, but not until it is clear that no purchaser for them is to be found. As soon as they have recovered, they must serve to pay off their fare, unless they have the means immediately to discharge the debt.

It often happens that whole families — husband, wife, and children — being sold to different purchasers, become separated, especially when they cannot pay any part of the passage money. When either the husband or the wife has died at sea, having come more than halfway, then the surviving spouse must pay not only his or her fare, but must also pay for or serve out the fare of the deceased.

When both parents have died at sea, having come more than halfway, then their children, especially when they are still young and have nothing to pawn or cannot pay, must be responsible for their own fares as well as those of their parents, and must serve until they are twenty-one years old. Once free of service, they receive a suit of clothing as a parting gift, and if it has been so stipulated the men get a horse and the women a cow.

When a servant in this country has the opportunity to get married he has to pay £5 to £6, that is, 30 to 36 florins for every year that he would still have had to serve. But many who must purchase and pay for their brides in this manner come to regret their purchases later. They would just as soon surrender their damnably expensive wares again and lose their money into the bargain.

No one in this country can run away from a master who has treated him harshly and get far. For there are regulations and laws that ensure that runaways are certainly and quickly recaptured. Those who arrest or return a fugitive get a good reward. For every day that someone who runs away is absent from his master he must as a punishment do service an extra week, for every week an extra month, and for every month a half year. But if the master does not want to take back the recaptured runaway, he is entitled to sell him to someone else for the period of as many years as he would still have had to serve.[6]

Occupations vary, but work is strenuous in this new land; and many who have just come into the country at an advanced age must labor hard for their bread until they die. I will not even speak of the young people. Most jobs involve cutting timber, felling oak trees, and levelling, or as one says there, clearing, great tracts of forest, roots and all. Such forest land, having been cleared in this way, is then laid out in fields and meadows. From the best wood that has been felled people construct railings or fences around the new fields. Inside these, all meadows, all lawns, gardens, and orchards, and all arable land are surrounded and enclosed by thickly cut wood planks set in zigzag fashion one above the other. And thus cattle, horses, and sheep are confined to pasture land.

Our Europeans who have been purchased must work hard all the time. For new fields are constantly being laid out; and thus they learn from experience that oak tree stumps are just as hard in America as they are in Germany. In these hot regions there is particularly fulfilled in them that with which the Lord God afflicted man in the first book of Moses, on account of his sin and disobedience, namely: "Thou shalt eat thy bread in the sweat of thy brow." Thus let him who wants to earn his piece of bread honestly and in a Christian manner and who can only do this by manual labor in his native country stay *there* rather than come to America.

For, in the first place, things are no better in Pennsylvania.

[6] For fugitives, *see* C. A. Herrick, *White Servitude in Pennsylvania* (Philadelphia, 1926), pp. 217 ff.

However hard one may have had to work in his native land, conditions are bound to be equally tough or even tougher in the new country. Furthermore the emigrant has to undertake the arduous voyage, which means not only that he must suffer more misery for half a year than he would have to suffer doing the hardest labor, but also that he must spend approximately two hundred florins which no one will refund to him. If he has that much money, he loses it; if he does not have it, he must work off his debt as a slave or as a miserable servant. So let people stay in their own country and earn their keep honestly for themselves and their families. Furthermore, I want to say that those people who may let themselves be talked into something and seduced into the voyage by the thieves of human beings are the biggest fools if they really believe that in America or Pennsylvania roasted pigeons are going to fly into their mouths without their having to work for them.

How sad and miserable is the fate of so many thousand German families who lost all the money they ever owned in the course of the long and difficult voyage, many of whom perished wretchedly and had to be buried at sea and who, once they have arrived in the new country, saw their old and young separated and sold away into places far removed one from the other! The saddest aspect of all this is that in most instances parents must give away their young children getting nothing in return. For such children are destined never to see or recognize parents, brothers, and sisters again, and, after they have been sold to strangers, are not brought up in any sort of Christian faith.

In Pennsylvania there exist so many varieties of doctrines and sects that it is impossible to name them all. Many peo-

ple do not reveal their own particular beliefs to anyone.
Furthermore there are many hundreds of adults who not only
are unbaptized, but who do not even want baptism. Many
others pay no attention to the Sacraments and to the Holy
Bible, or even to God and His Word. Some do not even believe in the existence of a true God or Devil, Heaven or Hell,
Salvation or Damnation, the Resurrection of the Dead, the
Last Judgment and Eternal Life, but think that everything
visible is of merely natural origin. For in Pennsylvania not
only is everyone allowed to believe what he wishes; he is
also at liberty to express these beliefs publicly and freely.

Thus when young people not raised in the fundamentals
of religion must go into service for many years with such
freethinkers and unbelievers and are not permitted by these
people to attend any church or school, especially when they
live far away from them, then such innocent souls do not
reach a true knowledge of the Divine and are brought up like
heathen or Indians.

The ocean voyage is sometimes dangerous for those people
who bring money and effects with them from home, because
at sea much is often spoiled by inrushing water. And sometimes they are robbed on board by dishonest people. Thus
such once-wealthy folk are to have really unhappy experiences.

As an example, let me tell the sad story of a man from
Württemberg. Late in the year 1753 Bailiff Daser, well
known to us at home, arrived in Philadelphia in a miserable
and unhappy state, having come from Nagold with his wife
and eight children. Not only had he been robbed on sea to
the tune of 1,800 florins, but on account of these thefts he
and the English ship's captain got involved in a great law-

suit at Philadelphia. Litigation brought him no gain. On the contrary, he had to pay costs and thus lost a great deal more. Mr. Daser had to pay 600 florins to cover the passage for himself and his family. Since, however, he had been robbed of his money, all his effects, including his boxes, were publicly auctioned off for a trifling sum at a *vendue*, or public auction. Thus he and his family found themselves in even more miserable circumstances.

When at this point he wanted to borrow some money in order to buy a plantation, he was shamefully cheated by his creditor. He had made an agreement with this man, to pay him back the borrowed sum within two years. But the person who drew up the *Obligation*, or bond, as it is known there, wrote, as the result of an intentional slip of the tongue by the unscrupulous creditor, "two days" instead of "two years." Mr. Daser signed the agreement not realising that he was signing his own doom, since he knew no English. The game was played in such a way that since he did not repay the money within two days, all he owned was sold, even the shirt from his very back. Actually he had not even received the money in the first place thanks to the creditor's negligence and his various subterfuges.

Indeed, he would probably have ended up in prison, or been forced to sell his children, if, through my intercession, he had not been saved by Captain von Diemer, who always showed great and laudable concern for Germans. The same Captain von Diemer out of charity then supplied Daser and his family with food, money, beds, and living quarters until the end of the trial. He also gave security for him, so that Mr. Daser did not have to go to debtors' prison. When I departed Captain von Diemer promised Mr. Daser and me, with hand

and mouth, to help take care of the Daser family and their needs as long as he lived. During a period of eight weeks, Mr. Daser took his meals in our house, and slept there, too. But, in truth, because of the many sad misfortunes he had suffered, he became very despondent and half lost his mind. His two oldest unmarried daughters and his oldest son were forced to go into service shortly before my departure, each bound by written contract for three years.

I want to take this opportunity to relate some curious and most unfortunate instances of shipwreck. On St. James's Day in 1754, a ship with some 360 souls on board, mainly Württemberger, Durlacher, and Palatines, was driven onto a rock at night by a storm between Holland and Old England. It received three shocks, each time accompanied by loud crashes. Finally it came apart lengthwise underneath. So much water rushed in that the ship started to sink early the next morning.

When the peril was at its greatest and people tried to save themselves, sixty-three persons jumped into one boat. Since this boat was already overloaded, and since yet another person swam to it and held on, it was impossible to drive him off in any other way than by chopping off his hands; so that he had to drown. Another person is supposed to have jumped onto a barrel which had fallen out of the great ship, in order to save himself in that way. But the barrel capsized at once and sank with him.

The people who remained on board the great ship, however, held on some to the rigging, some to the masts. Many stood deep in water, clapping their hands together over their heads, and crying together in an undescribably piteous manner. From the boat one could eventually see the great ship sink with three hundred souls aboard before one's very eyes. However, merciful God sent help, in the form of an English ship in the vicinity, to the rest who had saved themselves in the boat. This took them aboard in their great peril after their shipwreck, and brought them back to land. This great misfortune would not even have become known in Germany, had the ship perished during the night with all aboard.

The following unfortunate sea voyage involving many Germans has hardly or not at all become known in Germany. In 1752 a ship arrived in Philadelphia from Holland which had taken an entire half year to make the crossing. This ship had been battered by many storms during the entire winter and was unable to land, until at last another better ship came to help it in its miserable, starved-out, and half-wrecked state. This ship was able to bring 21 out of approximately 340 persons to Philadelphia. Not only had these been at sea for a full half year, and driven by the storm onto the coast of Ireland, but most people aboard had died of starvation. They had lost mast and sails, captain and mates. And the rest would never have reached land, if God had not come to their aid with another ship and had thus guided them here.

Another unfortunate sea voyage has probably also not become known in Germany. Some years ago an entire ship full of Germans is supposed to have been lost at sea. These people, too, were reported to have come to Philadelphia. But no one ever heard anything about them except that a description of this same ship was sent from Holland to the merchants of Philadelphia. News of such totally lost and wrecked ships is not publicized in Germany lest people be frightened away from the voyage, and prevented from making it.

I find it impossible to hold back what I heard from a reliable source in Pennsylvania by means of a bundle of letters posted at sea on the tenth of December 1754 that reached me on the first of September 1755. In these letters I am told in piteous fashion that in the autumn of the year just past (1754), once again more than 22,000 souls arrived in Philadelphia alone, a great burden to the country. Most of them were Württemberger, for at that time there took place a big emigration from Württemberg. The rest were Palatines, Durlacher, and Swiss. They were so miserably sick and wretched that once again most people had to sell their children on account of great poverty. Such a great mass of people imposed a great burden on the land, especially the multitude of the sick, of whom many daily continue to fill the graves.

While I was in the country, twenty to twenty-four ships full of people arrived in Philadelphia alone during the autumn of every year. Within the space of four years the city was invaded by more than 25,000 souls. This figure is in addition to those who died at sea or during the voyage, and does not count those ships full of people that sailed to other English colonies, that is, to New York, Boston, Maryland, Nova Scotia, and Carolina. Thus these colonies were filled up and people as people in the city of Philadelphia became worthless.

But the fact that so many still go to America and especially to Pennsylvania is to be blamed on the swindles and persuasions practised by so-called Newlanders. These thieves of human beings tell their lies to people of various classes and professions, among whom may be found many soldiers, scholars, artists, and artisans. They abduct people from their

Princes and Lords and ship them to Rotterdam or Amsterdam for sale. There they get three florins, or one ducat, from the merchant, for each person ten years or older. On the other hand the merchants get from sixty to seventy or eighty florins for such a person in Philadelphia, depending on the debts that said person has incurred on the voyage.

If such a Newlander has gathered together a transport and does not want to go to America himself, he stays behind, and spends the winter in Holland or elsewhere. In the spring he once more collects money in advance from his merchants, for the purchase of human beings. Then he begins to travel again, pretending to have come from Pennsylvania in order to buy all kinds of merchandise and to export it back there.

Often the Newlanders claim to have the authorization of the American government and of their fellow-countrymen in America to collect legacies belonging to these people. They also say that they want to take this certain and good opportunity to invite the friends, brothers and sisters, and even the fathers and mothers of those in America to join them. And it frequently happens that such old people follow their relatives, persuaded into the hope of finding better living conditions.

The Newlanders try to make these old people leave the country so that they can lure other people to go along with them. And so they pull the wool over the eyes of many who say that if such and such relatives would only come along, then they would be willing to risk the trip. This sort of enticement takes various forms. A favorite method is for these thieves of human beings to show the poor people money that, however, turns out to be nothing more than bait from Holland for human beings, and thus accursed blood-money.

Sometimes these thieves of human beings are able to talk persons of special rank, such as nobles or skilled or learned people, into making the trip. If these folk are able neither to pay their passage nor to give security, then they, just like the common poor folk, are not allowed to leave the ship, and must stay aboard until somebody comes and buys them from the ship's captain. And when they are finally let off, then they have to serve the lords and masters who purchased them, just as if they were common wage-laborers.

Their rank, skill and learning does not help them at all. For in America only workmen and artisans are needed. And the worst of it is that such people, not used to this kind of work, are beaten like cattle until they have learned hard labor. For this reason several people, finding themselves so wretchedly cheated by the Newlanders, have committed suicide. Others have fallen into such a state of despair that no one could any longer be of help to them. Still others have run away and have subsequently fared even worse than before.

It often happens that the merchants in Holland make a secret agreement with the captain and the Newlanders. This stipulates that the latter sail the fully-loaded ships not to Pennsylvania where these people want to go but to another place in America where they calculate they can sell their human cargo for a better price. In this way many who already have acquaintances or even perhaps friends, brothers, and sisters in Pennsylvania, to whose help and care they had been looking forward, are painfully hurt by being separated from their families and friends whom because of such godless misrouting they will never get to see again, either in this or that country. Thus both in Holland and at sea one has to put oneself into the hands of the wind and the captain; since at sea no one knows for certain just where the ship is proceeding. The blame for this rests with the Newlanders, and with a few unscrupulous dealers in human flesh in Holland.

Many people going to Philadelphia entrust the remains of the money they are able to bring away from home to these Newlanders. These thieves, however, often remain in Holland along with the money. Or they proceed from Holland on board another ship to a different English colony; so that the poor defrauded people, when they get to America, have no other recourse but to go into service, or to sell their children, if they have any, in order to get away from the ship.

Let me illustrate this by a curious example. In 1753 a noble lady, N.N., arrived in Philadelphia with two half-grown daughters and a young son. In the course of the Rhine journey this lady had made a loan of more than 1,000 reichsthaler to a Newlander otherwise well known to her. This villain remained in Holland along with the money after the departure of the lady's ship. Thus she was put into a position of such great want and need that her two daughters were forced to go into service. The same poor lady sent her son back across the ocean in the spring of the following year in order to locate the man who had stolen her money. But by the time of my departure in 1754 no one had heard anything of this man. Indeed, it was said that the young man looking for him had lost his life in the course of his search.

It is, by the way, impossible to touch on all the circumstances here. Besides, I am absolutely certain that those Newlanders or thieves of human beings who return never tell others the whole story and the real truth about such a miserable, difficult, and in the bargain highly dangerous voyage. When the Newlanders leave Pennsylvania or one of the other English colonies they are often given many letters to take along. When they get to Holland with these letters they have them broken open, or break them open themselves. And if someone has written in lamentation and told the truth, then such a letter is either rewritten or even thrown away.

In Pennsylvania I heard from the very lips of such thieves of human beings that in Holland there are many Jews who for a small fee are able to reproduce all seals and who can perfectly imitate all handwritings on demand. They are able to reproduce all strokes and letters, all signs and special features so faithfully that the person whose handwriting they have imitated must himself admit that it is indeed his own hand. Using such tricks they are able to cheat even people who are not gullible; and on those they practice their evil tricks all the more covertly. They themselves tell their intimates that this sort of thing is the best way of easily persuading people to leave for America.

They almost succeeded in deceiving me. For in Holland they tried to see to it that I should not leave America for good; and they attempted to use trickery and force in order to talk me into returning to England and America. These same merchants tried to convince me verbally in Rotterdam, as well as in writing from Amsterdam, that my wife and child with my sister-in-law and many of my countrymen had embarked for Philadelphia last summer with the year's final transport. In the course of this attempt they told me in great detail the names of my wife, my child and myself, as well as their height and their age. They also said that my wife had stated that her husband had been an organist in Pennsylvania for four years. They also showed me my wife's name in a letter and told me with what ship and captain they had sailed from Amsterdam; and how my wife had been accommodated in berth Number Twenty-Two with four other women.

All of this made me extraordinarily confused and irresolute. I showed them my wife's letters in which she clearly indicated that she would never go to America without me; that on the contrary she was expecting me with longing; and that she had once again received news from me to the effect that I had decided, God willing, to return to Germany during the next year. For all those reasons I could not possibly believe what they were telling me. This put me into such a state of consternation that I did not know what I ought to believe or do. At last, after mature deliberation, and without a doubt of the intent of Divine direction, I decided to complete my journey, in God's name, especially since I had already carried out the major part of it, that is, 1,400 hours, and had reached Germany.

In this I succeeded, and thus, thanks be to God, I escaped this great temptation. For I found that what these people had tried to tell and show me about my family in Holland was not true, since I encountered my wife and child happily at home. Had I believed these seducers of the people and returned by sea to England and America instead of coming home, this news might perhaps not have become so quickly known. In fact, my family and I would hardly or not at all have met again in this world.

The above mentioned thieves of human beings, as I found out afterwards, had described me and my wife completely and by name to the merchants in Holland. And the Newlanders for the second time tried to wheedle my wife into going to America. They doubtless thought that once I had left America I would reveal their whole bag of tricks as well as the miserable condition of the great mass of unfortunate families who had gone out there, and would in this way do great harm to their transports and their trafficking in human flesh.

At this point I must mention something that I forgot to relate before. As soon as the ships transporting people from Europe have anchored at Philadelphia, that is, the following morning, all male persons fifteen years or older are unloaded from the ship and put on to a boat. Then they are conducted two by two into town to the courthouse or city hall. There they must take the oath of allegiance to the Crown of Great Britain.[7] When they have done this, they are taken back to the ships. Only then does the commerce in human beings begin, as I described it earlier.

I want to add only one other thing, namely, that when persons are purchased they are asked for neither discharge papers nor references. If someone has escaped the hangman and has the rope still dangling around his neck or left both his ears in Europe, there would not on that account exist any obstacles for him in Pennsylvania. If, however, he indulges in wrongdoing once again, there is no hope for him. Thus Pennsylvania is an ideal country for gallows-and-wheel customers.

[7] The form of the oath is given in Ralph B. Strassburger, *Pennsylvania German Pioneers* (Norristown, 1934), I, 3–6.

II
DESCRIPTION OF THE PROVINCE
OF PENNSYLVANIA

II

DESCRIPTION OF THE PROVINCE
OF PENNSYLVANIA

Pennsylvania is one of the English settlements or colonies in North America. It borders on the sea, and is situated in the center of the rest of the English colonial territories. For it has above it, in the north, Nova Scotia, New England, New York, and New Jersey; and below it, in the south, Maryland, Virginia, Carolina, and Georgia. The distance from the city of London to the point where one loses sight of Old England is reckoned at 325 English miles; then from land to land, that is from the last sign of land in Old England to the first of Pennsylvania, 3,600 such miles; thence to Philadelphia 125 miles — altogether 4,050 English miles, or 1,350 German or rather Swabian hours. Three English miles add up to one Swabian hour, twenty-five such hours add up to one degree, just like French land-miles.

When ships approach this province, they sail out of the sea into the great river. This is a large bay made by the Delaware River, or rather it is really the Delaware River itself, which is very broad here. Proceeding to Philadelphia by this route one notices large stretches of even country with woods here and there on both sides of the bay.

The exit from the sea and the entrance into the great bay is in a northwesterly direction. The Delaware River in its lower part separates, at the point where one enters it, the two colonies of Pennsylvania and Maryland one from the other, Maryland on the left hand, Pennsylvania on the right. From the bay one can already see many high mountains, especially the Blue Mountains. And on one's left hand one can see tall and exceedingly beautiful cedar trees upon these mountains. The bay, however, which down below at the entrance from the sea is so broad that one can hardly see land on either side, becomes narrower and narrower; so that at Philadelphia the Delaware is only approximately one half-hour broad. Here low and high tide occur twice every twenty-four hours.

Philadelphia is situated, as just reported, 125 English miles or 40 hours' journey from the open sea. It is placed on a height in the interior, hard by the said river, into which most of the other streams of this colony empty. The rest flow into the other great principal river of Pennsylvania, the Susquehanna, which empties into Chesapeake Bay. From Philadelphia one can glimpse the open sea through a telescope.

Philadelphia is the capital of Pennsylvania. All sorts of commercial activity are carried on there. The city is very large and beautiful, and laid out in regular lines, with broad avenues and many cross-streets. All houses are built up to the fourth floor of stone or brick, and are roofed with cedarwood shingles. It takes almost a whole day to walk around the city; and every year approximately three hundred new houses are built. It is thought that in time Philadelphia will become one of the world's largest cities. The principal language is English; and so is the law of the land. The city has neither walls nor ramparts, since these are considered unnecessary. On both sides of the city there are rivers crowded with shipping, toward the east, the above-mentioned Delaware, toward the north, the Schuylkill. Both empty into the bay below the city.

Many large and small merchant ships are being built at the water's edge. The trade of this city and of this province with other countries and colonies shows a marked increase from year to year. Exports comprise for the most part fruit, flour, corn, tobacco, honey, many varieties of hides, various kinds of valuable furs, flax, and especially a great deal of flaxseed or linseed. Also finely cut lumber, horses, and all kinds of tame and wild animals. In exchange for this, ships coming from afar bring all kinds of goods, such as: various wines (Spanish, Portuguese, and German) of which a measure of the best costs one reichsthaler and of the worst, one gulden. Also spices, sugar, tea, coffee, rice, rum (a spirit distilled from sugar and molasses), fine china vessels, Dutch and English cloth, leather, linen cloth, fabrics, silks, damask, velvet, etc.

Already it is really possible to obtain all the things one can get in Europe in Pennsylvania, since so many merchant ships arrive there every year. Ships come in from Holland, Old and New England, Scotland, Ireland, Spain, Portugal, Maryland, New York, Carolina, and the West and East Indies. In Pennsylvania, the term West Indies is understood to include both Spanish and Portuguese America, as well as the islands, whether they belong to the English or to other nations.

In Philadelphia there is a newly built magnificent Court House, or City Hall, very tall, with four doors and four entrances. It is one hundred feet long and one hundred feet wide, stands detached from other buildings and has high

English plate glass windows on its four sides. In this same city there are already eight churches — three English, three German, one Swedish, and one belonging to the Quakers. In the last-named one can often hear and see a woman preaching in English; but no one in the meeting can be heard singing, since the Quakers do not approve of music. When the sermon has come to an end, anyone who has objections to it steps forward and expresses his opinion. On these occasions one can often hear two persons disputing in front of the whole assemblage; and this sometimes takes longer than the sermon.

A school where several languages are taught has already been established in Philadelphia. For in this city and in this part of the country one can see people from every part of the entire world, especially Europeans, of whom there are more than a hundred thousand. The greatest number of inhabitants of Pennsylvania is German. In the above-mentioned school many Germans pursue studies in the different languages.

In Philadelphia's courthouse, the principal courts are in session four times a year; and these are open to the public in all cases coming before them. On court days young and old may enter the chamber and may listen to the cross-examinations and to the judgments, which often cause the listeners to burst into uproarious laughter.

Here I want to adduce only one of many examples. Once the following case came before the court. An unmarried female, who had gotten herself pregnant, wanted the man who was responsible for a husband. She testified that he had forced her to submit to him. When both parties were asked to appear before the court and were closely cross-examined, the man was willing neither to listen to nor to answer questions. Rather, he merely stared impassively at the court officials, whatever they might be asking or saying, since he had been instructed to do so by his lawyers. When this game had been played long enough and when he was supposed to go off to prison — and this was shouted into his ears — he suddenly recovered his hearing, excused himself, asked for forgiveness, and spoke as follows.

When he had raped the woman, she had cried out so horribly that he had lost his hearing as a consequence. When he said this the woman started up and said: "O, you godless villain, how can you say this? You remember, I didn't say a word then." Which he then admitted and said that this was indeed true, that it was just this confession that he wanted from her. "Why hadn't she cried out?" he asked. There were enough other people sleeping in the house that same night to have heard her. Whereupon she answered that if she had thought that this time she would become pregnant, then she would certainly have cried for help. At this young and old broke into great laughter; and the man was at once acquitted and set free.

Here is another story, one that did not come out so well for the man involved. A purchased serving-maid in an English house became pregnant by the master's manservant. When she could not hide her condition any longer, she reported it herself to the master who was a J.P., which was tantamount to being a judge or magistrate.[1] The master was very angry about the matter. But finally, out of pity, he said to the maid that she would be doing herself a great deal of

---

[1] Mittelberger used the term *Justus* where obviously Justice of the Peace was intended. In the translation, J.P. will be used.

harm were she to charge this dissolute rake with being the father of her child. For in the first place he would not be free from service for a long time to come. Furthermore, he did not own a cent. Moreover, as she knew herself, he was not a provider, and thus was not in any position to maintain her and her child in the future. If, however, she wanted his counsel, he was willing to give her a piece of better advice, so that she as well as her child would be taken care of in time to come.

The unhappy serving-maid was very anxious to hear this piece of advice. She promised the master that she would accept it, and begged him most anxiously to tell her the nature of his counsel. The master thereupon forbade her strictly to reveal what he was about to tell her, and said that she should merely go and name as the father another single man known to her as having a good name and great wealth. But to a different J.P., since he, as her master, might be regarded as too partisan in this matter. And she would have to stick by her story. The maid liked this piece of advice, and had an even better idea. She went to another J.P., reported to him that she was pregnant, and maintained that it was her master himself who was the father of her child. Moreover, she said she could state this with certainty, in spite of the fact that her master would not admit it. And since he was now a widower, she claimed that he could and had to maintain her.

The J.P. then exacted an oath from her according to English law, or the law of the land, by making her kiss the Bible. As soon as this had happened, he had the master reported by her brought before him at once, as is the custom of the country, and examined him. However, since the master did not want to confess anything, he had to go to prison and had to stay there until he had promised in writing either to marry his pregnant maidservant or to pay her the sum of £200, which in German currency comes to 1,200 gulden. Under these circumstances he chose to keep his maidservant rather than to give her 1,200 florins, and was married to her at once. He himself acknowledged this as right, since it was he who had advised her to report an innocent man as the father of her child. Similar cases frequently happen in this country, especially since the women possess considerable privileges and liberties.

To come back to Pennsylvania again. It offers people more freedom than the other English colonies, since all religious sects are tolerated there. One can encounter Lutherans, members of the Reformed Church, Catholics, Quakers, Mennonites or Anabaptists, Herrenhüter or Moravian Brothers, Pietists, Seventh-Day Adventists, Dunkers, Presbyterians, New-born, Freemasons, Separatists, Freethinkers, Jews, Mohammedans, Pagans, Negroes, and Indians. But the Evangelicals and the Reformed constitute the majority. There are several hundred unbaptized people who don't even wish to be baptized. Many pray neither in the morning nor in the evening, nor before or after meals. In the homes of such people are not to be found any devotional books, much less a Bible. It is possible to meet in one house, among one family, members of four or five or six different sects.

Freedom in Pennsylvania extends so far that everyone's property — commercial, real estate, and personal possessions — is exempt from any interference or taxation. For owning a hundred morgen of land one is assessed an annual tax of not more than one English shilling. This is called ground-rent or quit-rent.[2] One shilling is worth approximately eighteen kreuzer in German money. What is peculiar is that single men and women must pay two to five shillings annually, in proportion to their earnings, the reason for this being that they have none but themselves to look after. In Philadelphia the money raised in this way is used to purchase lights by which the streets of the city are illuminated every night.

This province was granted by the King of England to a distinguished Quaker named Penn. That is how it got its name. The young lords, the Penns, are still alive, residing not in America but in London, in Old England. In 1754 a young Lord Penn visited the country.[3] He renewed and confirmed all previously granted privileges with his signature, and also made many grants to the Indians or savages.

In Pennsylvania no profession or craft needs to constitute itself into a guild. Everyone may engage in any commercial or speculative ventures, according to choice and ability. And if someone wishes or is able to carry on ten occupations at one and the same time, then nobody is allowed to prevent it. And if, for example, a lad learns his skill or craft as an apprentice or even on his own, he can then pass for a master and may marry whenever he chooses. It is an admirable thing that young people born in this new country are easily taught, clever, and skillful. For many of them have only to look at and examine a work of skill or art a few times before being able to imitate it perfectly. Whereas in Germany it would take most people several years of study to do the same. But in America many have the ability to produce

[2] The morgen was a unit of area slightly less than an acre. 100 morgen were approximately 90 acres.
[3] The Penns held the title of Lord Proprietors of Pennsylvania.

even the most elaborate objects in a short span of time. When these young people have attended school for half a year, they are generally able to read anything.

The province of Pennsylvania is a healthy one; for the most part it has good soil, good air and water, lots of high mountains, and lots of flat land. There are many woods, and where these are not inhabited, there is natural forest through which flow many small and large rivers. The land is also very fertile, and all kinds of grain flourish.

The province is well populated, inhabited far and wide, and various new towns have been founded here and there, namely Philadelphia, Germantown, Lancaster, Reading, Bethlehem, and New Frankfort. Many churches have also been built in this region, but it takes a great many people two, three, four, five, and up to ten hours to get to church. But everyone, men and women, rides to church on horseback, even though they could walk the distance in half an hour. This is also customary at weddings and funerals. At times at such formal country weddings or funerals, it is possible to count up to four hundred or five hundred persons on horseback. One can easily imagine that on such occasions, just as at Holy Communion, nobody appears in black crepe or in a black cloak.

I should like to describe the funeral customs in greater detail. When someone has died, especially in the country, where people live far apart from one another, separated by plantations and forests, the actual time of burial is first announced only to the four closest neighbors of the deceased, each of whom in turn passes the information along to his closest neighbor. In such a manner the news of that kind of a funeral spreads through a radius of more than fifty English miles within twenty-four hours. Then, whenever possible, each family sends at least one representative, riding on horseback, to the funeral at the proper time. While these people are assembling, those present are handed pieces of good cake on a large tin platter. Aside from that everyone gets a goblet of well-warmed West Indian rum, to which are added lemons, sugar, and juniper berries, which makes a good combination. After this the guests are also offered warmed sweet cider.

This particular American funeral custom is just like the European wedding custom. When almost all the people are there and the time of the funeral approaches, the corpse is carried to the general burial ground. When that is too far away, burial takes place in the dead person's own field. Those people who have previously assembled ride silently behind the coffin. Sometimes one may count from one to four hundred persons in such a procession. The coffins are all made out of beautiful walnut wood, stained quite brown, and shiny with varnish. Wealthy people attach four beautifully worked brass handles to the coffin. By these one can take hold of the coffins to carry them to the grave. If the deceased has been a young man his coffin is carried by four maidens; if a young girl, by four unmarried youths.

In this country it is no rarity to find many totally unlearned men preaching in the open fields. For the sectaries say and believe that today's scholars are no longer apostles and have turned their learning into a mere trade. Nevertheless, there are at present many fine preachers in Pennsylvania who through God's mercy and their own indefatigable zeal have converted many to the Christian faith. I can myself testify to the manner in which our Evangelical ministers have baptized and confirmed many adults, both white and Black. Many people come to watch such ceremonies when they take place.

Alas, among the preachers there are also several quite irritating ones who offend many people, besides causing much annoyance to our ministers. I will cite one example of such an objectionable preacher. His name was Alexander. At a gathering of young farmers from the township of Oley with whom he had been carousing he announced that with his sermon he would so move the people standing in front of him that all of them would begin to cry, but at the very same time all of those standing behind him would start laughing. He wagered these same young farmers a considerable sum that he would be able to do this. And on a certain agreed day he appeared at a churchmeeting, stationed himself in the midst of the assemblage, and began to preach with a great deal of power and emotion. When he saw that his listeners had become so moved that they began to cry, he put his hands behind him, pulled his coat-tails apart, and revealed through a pair of badly torn breeches his bare behind, which he scratched with one hand during this demonstration. At this those who were standing behind him could not help roaring with laughter; and so he won his bet. An account of this disgusting incident appeared both in the German and English newspapers of Philadelphia.

The sectarians often said to the people of our faith: such men are false prophets who go around in sheep's clothing, but are ravenous wolves underneath. They are a great source of difficulty and annoyance for all the upstanding teachers and for all good pastors and ministers in this country.

Apart from these, there are at present many good English, Swedish, Dutch, and German ministers of the Lutheran and Reformed churches in Pennsylvania, of whom I knew the following very well: among the English are the three brothers Dennent and Mr. Datt; and three Swedish preachers were very closely associated with ours and held annual joint conferences with them. The German-Evangelical-Lutheran preachers are the following: Mr. Muhlenberg, Senior, in the township of Providence and New Hanover, Mr. Brunnholtz, in Philadelphia, Mr. Handschuh in Germantown, Mr. Kurtz in Tulpehocken, Mr. Wagner in Reading, Mr. Heinzelmann in Philadelphia, Mr. Schultz, Mr. Weygand, Mr. Schrenk, and Mr. Schartel in the Blue Mountains, and Mr. Gerock at Lancaster. The Reformed ministers are: Mr. Schlatter, Mr. Steiner, Mr. Siebele, Mr. Weiss, Mr. Michael, Mr. Streiter, and Mr. Leidig — not to mention the Dutch and those whose names are unknown to me.

In Pennsylvania preachers receive no salary or tithes. Their total income is what they get annually from their church members, and that sum varies a good deal. For some heads of households annually contribute according to their means and of their own free will from two to six florins. Others, however, contribute very little. For baptisms, funerals, and weddings the contribution is generally a whole thaler. Preachers do not receive free lodging or other similar emoluments. But they are given many presents by penitents who confess to them.

Schoolteachers are in the same situation. Since the year 1754, however, England and Holland have annually contributed a large sum of money for the general benefit of the many poor in Pennsylvania and for the maintenance of six Reformed English churches and an equal number of Reformed English free schools. Many hundreds of children, however, are unable to go to school partly because the distances are too great and partly because of the extent of forest land they would have to traverse. Thus many planters lead a rather wild and heathenish life. The situation of rural churches and rural schools is similar. In general, churches and school houses are located only in those places where several neighbors or church members live close together.*

Throughout Pennsylvania the preachers do not have the power to punish anyone, or to force anyone to go to church. Nor can they give orders to each other, there being no consistory to impose discipline among them. Most preachers are engaged for the year, like cowherds in Germany; and when any one fails to please his congregation, he is given notice and must put up with it. So it is very difficult to be a conscientious minister; especially since one has to tolerate and suffer a great deal from so many hostile, and to some

---

* In an English publication dealing with the conditions of emigrants who settled in Pennsylvania, Virginia, and Maryland, the following is reported, among other things. It appears, from the most trustworthy reports we have of these provinces, that in the course of the last few years there has been a tremendous increase in the numbers of emigrants there. The major proportion of these comprises Palatines, Franconians, and Swiss. In the colony of Pennsylvania alone there are over 100,000, of whom 20,000 belong to the Reformed, nearly the same number to the Lutheran and approximately 1,700 to the Roman Catholic religion. The rest consists of Anabaptists, Moravians, Brethren of Zion, Rondorfers, and other Separatists. Since among the last nearly everyone is his own teacher, it is possible to say of them that they have a better knowledge of the tenets of their religion, if the inanities of these people deserve that name, than many of the other denominations. For though it is possible to encounter not a few devout and divinely enlightened Christians among the latter, the majority is sunk in the profoundest ignorance. The reason for this is the lack of a sufficient number of preachers and schoolteachers, for whose support the inhabitants do not have the means. The author of this publication concludes with the wish that the British nation might take to heart the spiritual as well as the material condition of its brethren, and might help to put them in the position of forming a constant bulwark in America against all its enemies.

extent vile, sects. Even the most exemplary preachers, especially in rural districts, are often reviled, laughed at and mocked by young and old, like Jews. I myself would therefore rather be the humblest cowherd at home than be a preacher in Pennsylvania. Such outrageous coarseness and rudeness result from the excessive freedom in that country, and from the blind zeal of the many sects. Liberty in Pennsylvania does more harm than good to many people, both in soul and in body. They have a saying there: Pennsylvania is heaven for farmers, paradise for artisans, and hell for officials and preachers.

Hamilton, the man who was Governor while I was there, resided in Philadelphia. Every six years a new governor is chosen by the King and Parliament in England, and is sent to Pennsylvania to rule in the name of the King. But the province itself and most of the revenues belong to a Quaker named Penn. That is why the city of Philadelphia and the whole region are heavily settled with Quakers.

Provisions are cheap in Pennsylvania. On the other hand, everything that has to be manufactured and brought into the country is three to four times as expensive as it is in Germany, with the exception of wood, salt, and sugar. Apart from these it is possible to purchase as much with one gulden in Germany as with four or five in Pennsylvania. Nevertheless, people are amply fed, especially on all sorts of grain which grows well there because the soil is virgin and rich. They grow chiefly rye, wheat, barley, oats, buckwheat, flax, hemp, cabbage, and turnips. They also raise good cattle, fast horses, and many bees. Sheep, bigger than those in Germany, generally produce two lambs a year. Almost everyone raises pigs and poultry, especially turkeys.

In this region chickens are not confined to coops or especially looked after during the night. But they sit summer and winter on trees near the houses. And every evening many trees are so weighted down with chickens that the boughs bend underneath them. Poultry is in no danger from beasts of prey, because every plantation owner has at least one very large dog roaming the estate.

In this province, even in the humblest or poorest houses, no meals are served without a meat course; and no one eats bread without butter or cheese, even though the bread is as good as ours. However, it is most annoying that nothing but salted meat is consumed during the summer, and fresh meat rarely during the winter. Because so much cattle is raised, meat is cheap. A pound of the best beef costs three kreuzer, a pound of pork and mutton two kreuzer and three hellers. Besides these one can buy various meats according to choice and for very little money, — namely venison, poultry, fish, and fowl. I do not believe that any country consumes more meat than Pennsylvania.

The English know little or nothing about eating soup. Their dessert always consists of bread, butter, and cheese. And because sugar, tea, and coffee are very cheap, they drink coffee and the like two or three times a day. A pound of coarse sugar costs ten kreuzer, the best, fifteen kreuzer; coffee costs the same, a pound of rice three kreuzer. All vegetables and garden produce are raised in abundance. A bushel of salt costs fifteen kreuzer. Timber and wood for fuel cost no one anything.

Twice a week it is market day in Philadelphia, and a great crowd of people gathers. The ordinary meat stalls are over one hundred feet in length, with all kinds of meat hanging

49

on both sides, all of which is bought and consumed by the numerous population. Not to mention the many kinds of fish, game, all sorts of poultry, and especially the marvelously large lobsters, each of whose claws is as big as a man's hand. I often saw turtles so big that a man could not carry more than a single one. A hen costs six kreuzer and eggs are sometimes to be had twenty for a batzen.[4] A turkey is worth twenty-four to thirty kreuzer, a bushel of rye two shillings, or thirty-six kreuzer, a bushel of good wheat three shillings, or fifty-four kreuzer.

There is enough fruit so that it can be cheaply sold. It is often exported to other regions, being transported by sea. All other goods, however, cost two to three times as much as they do in Germany, because they have to be brought in from so far. So that what can be purchased for one gulden in Germany costs four to five florins in Pennsylvania and the neighboring provinces. Domestic linen, which costs fifteen or eighteen kreuzer an ell in Germany, is worth forty kreuzer or even a gulden in these English colonies. A pair of man's shoes also costs two to three florins more than it does in Germany; likewise, a pair of stockings.

Many kinds of beverages are available in Pennsylvania and the other English colonies. First of all, excellent and salubrious water; secondly, people drink a mixture of three parts of water and one part of milk; thirdly, there is good cider; fourthly, small beer; fifth, delicious English beer, strong and sweet; sixth, so-called punch, made of three parts water and one part West Indian rum (where there is no rum, one can use brandy, but rum is much more pleasant), mixed in with sugar and lemon juice; seventh, sangaree,

[4] The batzen was a small German coin, now obsolete.

which is even more delicious to drink — this is made out of two parts of water and one of Spanish wine with sugar and nutmeg; and then, eighth, German and Spanish wines, which are obtainable in all taverns. According to my latest report one measure of this costs one reichsthaler. Mixed drinks are all drunk out of china vessels, called bowls, which have the same shape as soup plates.

All trades and professions bring in good money. No beggars are to be seen; for every township feeds and takes care of its poor. In the country people live so far apart that many have to walk a quarter or a half-hour just to reach their nearest neighbor. The reason for this is that many plantation owners have got fifty or one hundred, even two, three, up to four hundred morgen of land, laid out in orchards, meadows, fields, and forest. Usually such planters own from ten to twenty acres of orchards alone — from which a great deal of cider and brandy is derived.

Many plantation owners plant whole avenues of peach and cherry trees, stretching from one plantation to the next. These flourish in abundance. One kind of peach is red both inside and outside, as big as a lemon, but round and smooth, and ripe around St. Bartholomew's Day. There are also waxen yellow peaches, as well as red-striped and grass-green peaches. There is also one sort called cling-stone. They are very sweet, and are often preserved before they are entirely ripe, like cucumbers. There are few pears, and no damson plums — they will not thrive and are often spoiled by mildew.

Every plantation owner pastures his cattle, horses, and sheep on his own property, or lets them run about in the underbrush and has them brought in mornings and evenings in order to have the cows milked. Then he lets them go again the whole night through until morning. In this way the animals find their own food, and one doesn't have to feed them daily, as in Germany. And no cattle has to be stabled during the summers, except when cows are about to calve. But often, a cow with her calf is found wandering in the forest, or returns unexpectedly to the farm with her offspring. For all these reasons no shepherds or cowherds are needed, since all cattle and sheep are either confined to fenced-in fields, or left to run about in the woods where they find plenty of food, and in some places spoil much beyond what they consume.

In Pennsylvania's rural districts newborn children are sometimes not brought to church to be baptized until they are two weeks, several weeks, a quarter of a year or a half a year, sometimes even one year old. Often such big and strong children put up a fight against the minister or the baptist and cause much laughter. Pennsylvanian mothers are in the habit of suckling their restive children in church even while Holy Baptism is in progress. Also, many parents follow the custom of themselves acting as sponsors for their children, because they have no trust or confidence in other people when it comes to this important matter. One should not blame them for this in view of the fact that many people do not frankly express what they really believe.

Others, who are themselves baptized, nevertheless do not have their children baptized. When one asks them why, they answer: they neither see nor feel any difference between baptized and unbaptized young people. Also, that nobody keeps his baptismal vows and that it is therefore not necessary to pay the minister a thaler for the ceremony. In my school in Pennsylvania I encountered many adults of both sexes who, when I asked them whether they were baptized, answered: "No, what is the use of it?" Whereupon I tried to make them conscious of their unbelief by quoting Nicodemus's conversation with Jesus. Thus I brought many young people to a realization of the necessity for Holy Baptism; so that they became quite anxious about the matter and began to wish they were baptized. Some were eager to master the principal points of all the Evangelical Christian doctrines. This was something that many parents did not want to permit. They told me that they did not send their children to school in order to absorb religious beliefs, but only to acquire the necessary ability to read and write.

Plenty of wild black and white vines are to be found in Pennsylvania, as well as throughout North America, from Acadia to Mexico, growing in forests around oak trees, and along hedges. Many of these vines have the thickness of trees from the bottom up, and are often so plentifully hung with grapes that the boughs of the trees bend beneath them. At blossom time the grapes give off a strong odor. They are ripe in October. One can use them to make a little wine, but one has to add a great deal of sugar. Many grapes are brought to market in Philadelphia. Such grapes would be far better if the vines were cut, as in Europe. But people live too far apart; and the many wild animals and birds would do too much damage to the vines. Thus it is likely there will be no cultivation of vines for some time to come.

Sassafras trees, not to be found in Europe, are plentiful here. From their blossoms one can make the best sort of breast-tea. The wood and the roots are especially good for medicinal purposes. There are trees the thickness of a man.

Their leaves look and smell like laurel leaves; but the blossoms look golden yellow, just like primroses, but far more delicate in coloring. For my voyage home I gathered and took with me a bag of sassafras flowers or blossoms. They were the best medicine I had at sea.

There are many sugar trees * in this country, as thick and tall as oaks. In the spring, when they are in full sap, it is possible to tap the syrup. I tried this myself, and in March, when the trees began to flow, I bored a hole at the bottom of one through the bark and inserted a small tube made from a quill through which the syrup began to flow, just as when one is purifying brandy. Within a quarter of an hour I had a full glass of sugar-water. The people who collect that kind of syrup fill a kettle with it, and let the water boil till thick. When it cools off, it becomes like a kind of thick honey. Sugar trees are usually found in forests near brooks, and grow wild.

Many beautiful tulip trees † grow there. During the month of May when they are in blossom, they bear many flowers, colored a blazing yellow and red; and as natural as those grown from bulbs. The trees are as thick and tall as big cherry trees. I have observed yet another sort of tulip

* This species of tree has been described under the name of maple in the *History and Transactions of the French Colonies in North America* (p. 213). De Dièreville calls them wild fig trees.[5]

† The French in Louisiana call these tulip trees *Tulipier*, a species of laurel tree. See the book quoted above, p. 334.

[5] For the works cited in this and subsequent footnotes by the original editor, *see*: Pierre François Xavier Charlevoix, *Histoire et description générale de la Nouvelle France* (Paris, 1744; English trans. by J. G. Shea, New York, 1872); [N.] de Dièreville, *Relation du voyage du Port Royal de l'Acadie, ou de la Nouvelle France* (Rouen, 1708; English trans., London, 1714; condensed German trans., Göttingen, 1751). *See also* the Champlain Society edition of Dièreville (Toronto, 1933); Nicolas Denys, *Description géographique et histoire des costes de l'Amérique septentrionale* (Paris, 1672; English trans. by W. F. Ganong, Toronto, 1908).

trees with their blooms. These are planted in gardens, but are no larger than dwarfed fruit trees. They do not bloom until August and are colored a blazing white and red. No blossoms appear on the first and large kind of tulip tree for a period of twenty or more years.

Many other kinds and species of trees, flowers, and herbs, as well as of grain, are to be found in America. Among others, for example, there is the daisy, so common and for that reason so little esteemed at home. But in Pennsylvania it is as rare as the most beautiful and rarest flowers can be in Europe. For they plant it as a rare flower in their gardens. The juniper shrub is equally rare there, being held in higher esteem than rosemary with us. And juniper berries are sold for higher prices than peppercorns. Juniper shrubs are also cultivated in gardens. All other European flowers and shrubs are equally rare. So, what is of little value in Germany is very expensive and rare in America. On the other hand, what is not valued highly there is valuable in Germany. The Germans who have emigrated to America mourn after the good things they have lost by doing so, especially the Württemberger and the Rhinelander who miss the noble juice of the grape.

In all of Pennsylvania not a single meadow-saffron or "timeless flower," so-called, is to be seen in autumn time in the gardens and meadows. Wood grows quickly in the province; and it is much taller, though not as durable, as it is at home. This is a matter for great surprise, especially since the forests are very dense and consist of such beautiful, smooth, thick, and tall trees. Many kinds of trees grow there, mostly oaks that, however, are not as fruitful as those in Germany. Then there are also beech trees, but not many.

One rarely sees birches. But I did see some birch trees that were as tall and as thick as a sturdy oak tree.

I have already mentioned the poplars. Their wood is soft, and it looks as white as snow inside. There are many of them. Walnut trees are indescribably plentiful. Their beautiful wood, hard and the color of brown coffee, is both precious and useful. All sorts of fine and beautiful household furniture are made from it. When it has been cut, much of it is sent overseas to Holland, England, Ireland, and similar places, where it fetches a good price. These walnut trees bear nuts every year. They are the size of a medium-sized apple. A great deal of oil is made from them. Their bark and leaves are similar to those of our large nut trees.

One finds few German or large walnut trees planted there as yet. In the forests there are few hazelnut shrubs. But on the other hand, there is a great mass of chestnut trees. There are also many hickory nuts, larger than hazel nuts, but not highly valued. One does not see many Indian or wild cherry trees. I myself have gathered and eaten Indian cherries. They are, however, not as good as the European cherries. There are no thorn and sloe hedges in the Pennsylvania forests, and no hedge berries or the like.

Beautiful and excellent cedar trees are the greatest ornament of the forests. They grow mostly in the high mountains. Their wood has a strong smell, is as light as foam, and is especially valuable for the construction of organ pipes. For organ pipes made of cedar wood have a far finer and purer tone than those made of tin. I saw enough evidence of this fact. All houses in Philadephia are roofed with shingles made of cedar wood. Pelted by heavy rain, this wooden roof sounds like one made of copper or brass.

In springtime you do not see many May bugs in this country. But every five years there appears a horrible army of vermin called locusts, or *lockis.** They are slightly bigger than May bugs and can do great damage in the fields and the forests. One does not see red and white snails here. And frogs make a totally different sound. They don't quack; they yelp. And this yelping begins as early as March.

American birds are quite different from those in Europe. Only ravens, swallows, and little hedge sparrows are exactly like European birds. American birds are very wonderful. It is impossible to overpraise their beautiful colors and their lovely songs. First of all, there are yellow birds with black wings; secondly, red birds with black wings; thirdly, completely yellow birds; fourthly, starlings, bigger than ours, blue all over with red wings; fifthly, brilliantly red ones with plumes on their heads; sixthly, entirely blue ones; seventhly, white ones with black wings; eighthly, multi-colored ones; ninthly, grass-green ones, with red heads; tenthly, there is a pied species colored black and white. These birds can imitate the song and the whistling of all other birds; within a half-hour such a bird can imitate thirty birds one after the other.

There is also a kind of bird who during the summer calls very clearly all day long: "Get you gone. Get you gone." Another kind, heard mainly at night, calls. "Whip-poor-Will. Whip-poor-Will"; and is known by that name. In Pennsylvania one doesn't find storks, magpies, cuckoos, larks, yellow-hammers, nightingales, quail, thistle-birds, goldfinches, canaries, blackbirds, tomtits, robin-redbreasts, redwings,

---

* This creature seems to be a species of grasshopper. Perhaps the word *Lockis* is derived from *Locusta*.

and sparrows. It is possible that some Pennsylvanian birds bear some resemblance to the birds I just mentioned. But they are not completely similar, differing either in size, color, song, or something else. For instance, it is conceivable that one might take for a quail the Pennsylvanian bird who cries "Get you gone!" in almost the same cadence in which our quails call. But he has one thing our quail does not have, a little tail.

The most marvelous bird of all, not only in Pennsylvania but perhaps in the entire world, is a little bird rarely to be seen. This little bird is not even the size of a May bug. It is no bigger than a gold-crested wren. It glitters like gold, and sometimes it appears to be green, blue, and red. Its beak is a little long, and sharp as a needle; its feet are like very fine wire. It sips nothing but honey out of flowers, and that is why it is known as the sugar-bird.* It builds its nest

* Father Charlevoix describes the bird under the name of fly bird, and demonstrates that it is even more beautiful than the hummingbird. See the *History and Transactions of the French Colonies in North America* (published by Mezler), p. 248. But let us hear what yet another author has to say about this rare bird. This is M. de Dièreville in his *Voyage to Acadia*, which may be found in the Collection of Voyages published in Göttingen. On p. 237 he writes as follows:

Let us now discuss small birds, whose eggs do not stand in danger of pilfering since they are no bigger than hempseed. These are the eggs belonging to the hummingbirds or fly birds, the most beautiful birds in the whole world, with colors so brilliant that it seems as if certain portions — and especially the males under the throat — emit flashes of fire. It is impossible to imagine anything more varied and at the same time more brilliant than these colors. But these birds are only to be seen at that time of the year when flowers are in season. For like the bees they fly from one flower to the next, in order to sip the sweet nectar from the pale as well as the reddish ones.

They carry out all these different movements with the utmost speed; no other bird resembles them in this. And one can hardly see them as they whir through the air. They show the same nimbleness in everything they do. They do not, for example, land on the flowers in order to suck out the sweet nectar hidden in their delicate tubes. All they do is flap in some such place as the flower pots in a garden. And though the nest is no bigger than a cupping glass, there are generally four or five young in it. This bird moves its wings incredibly quickly, and makes a loud hissing sound with them. When these birds are not in flight, one can hear them singing most gracefully and prettily, if one is lucky enough to be quite close to them. I won't say how much great people are sometimes willing to pay for these birds. But they do not live long, as it is impossible to give them the food they require.

---

their wings around the flower incessantly and with such swiftness that it is impossible to describe it. The way in which nature, that wise artificer, formed the beak and tongue of these small birds is truly admirable. The beak, black and thin, and pointed almost perfectly straight, is about a finger's breadth in length; and the delicate, split tongue is perhaps twice as long. In inserting this into a flower and moving it constantly, they fill it with the sweet nectar contained in each calyx. This juice is subsequently brought to their little stomachs by means of a force peculiar to the tongue. It constitutes their sole nourishment.

They have a light grey belly, a silver green back, and a black tail shot through with white. Their black wings and feet are perfectly proportioned to their small body, which is no thicker than the tip of a child's finger. And this same bird is described in the following manner in the *Description of New Scotland* (8 vols., Frankfurt, 1750, p. 174):

Among all the birds to be found here the most curious is the *murmur* (hummingbird), of which there are two species. One is extraordinarily small, with all its feathers no larger than a small fly. The other makes a loud noise in one's ears, like the humming of a big gnat, which is not much louder. Its claws which are the length of a thumb, seem to be fine needles, as is its beak, which is merely the sheath of another beak that it extends and puts in the midst of flowers in order to extract honey from them. This is its nourishment.

In short, this creature deserves to be called the ornament of nature. This bird wears a black plume on its crest, which is of an extraordinary beauty. Its breast resembles the most beautiful rose color one can see anywhere, and its belly is as white as milk. Its back, wings and tail are colored the most beautiful grey, which can well be compared with roses, and they are shaded all around with a brilliant gold. Its down which can barely be seen and which covers its whole plumage, gives it so delicate an appearance that it resembles a flower. It resembles a wave. All this is so delicate and pretty that it beggars description.

In Pennsylvania masses of fish may be caught every spring in the Delaware and Schuylkill rivers. And lots of wild pigeons can be shot twice a year, that is, in spring when they migrate north, and late in the fall when they return to migrate south.* The fish ascend from the sea at their proper seasons; and those not caught return to sea again toward the end of May. These fish are one ell in length, and nearly one half-ell in breadth. Often so many are caught that some people salt a whole barrel or tub full of them, enough to last an entire year. When one wants to eat these fish, one puts them into fresh water over night. Then they are washed once more, and fried. The pigeons that have been shot are salted in the same manner and brought to the table in winter time.

There is no longer as great a quantity of wildfowl and game around Philadelphia as there used to be, since everybody is allowed to shoot what he wants. But the further one penetrates into the country, the less inhabited it is, and the more game of all kinds one encounters, especially birds. Many people in this province support themselves by hunting.

One comes across many kinds of snakes as well as many kinds of vermin in Pennsylvania, especially in the Blue Mountains. There, many a snake ten, twelve, fifteen to eighteen feet long has been observed and many people as well as animals have been fatally bitten by these terrible and vicious creatures. There are black and white snakes, grass-green ones, grey ones, and then again black ones with yellow stripes. Among all these rattlesnakes are the biggest and most dangerous. But in some ways black snakes (twelve to fifteen feet long and thick as an arm) can do even more

* About these pigeons, see the book just cited, p. 306.

harm, since they have a marvelous power to charm through their steady glance, which, once fixed upon it, forces any creature crossing their path, be it hare, bird or squirrel, down from the trees and towards them. Then they pounce upon it and devour it.*

They can climb the tallest oaks as well as other trees. They are also able to charm little children, who are compelled to stand stock-still in front of them. The children then begin to cry pitifully. And so it often happens that one can still save them, while the large snakes are still coiled in front of them. Some of the rattlesnakes are even bigger than the species hitherto mentioned. Many of them are over eighteen feet long, and as thick as a haypole. This kind of snake has a rattling tail at its rear end. With this it can rattle; and one can hear it from afar. These snakes also rattle when they are angry or when they catch sight of anyone. Each year the rattle-tail develops a new ring. These creatures have fishlike scales — black, blue, and green — and they look like mother-of-pearl. It has often happened to people living in the forests that snakes have crawled into their houses, even under their beds, until the people lying on the beds became too heavy for the snakes and the latter grew restless. Then one could chase them out and beat them to death.

Among the beauties of Pennsylvania are the fireflies that fly about in such numbers during the summertime that it appears to be snowing fire. Some years ago a newly arrived German got into a great fright over this. For when he was

---

* This account sounds rather strange, and I should be inclined to regard it as a fable palmed off on the author, had I not read the same account in the *Description of New Scotland,* which I cited above, pp. 213, 214. In this latter account, however, the power to charm is ascribed to the rattlesnakes, whereas our author attributes it to the black snakes.

working late in the fields one evening at firefly time and several of the fireflies flew to and fro about him (he was not familiar with them) our Honest Hans was scared out of his wits, dropped everything, and rushed home. When, full of fright, he got home to his family, he said in fear and trembling, "O, God, guard and protect us. How many fiery spirits are abroad in this country. O, God, if only I were back in Germany!"

The Blue Mountains of Pennsylvania are located about thirty hours' journey from Philadelphia. These mountains begin at the Delaware River and extend to the left of this clear across the country, reaching as far as the great Ohio River. The mountains are very high. One can already catch sight of them from Delaware Bay, before one has even reached Philadelphia. These Blue Mountains extend over forty hours' journey.

There are a great many savages or Indians who are in peaceful communication with the English. These live even beyond the Ohio and beyond the Hudson River on which Albany lies, that is, on both sides, right and left, of Pennsylvania. These two large rivers are about a hundred hours' journey from Philadelphia. These savages live in the bush in huts, away from the above-mentioned rivers, and indeed so far inland that no one is able to find the point to which their habitations extend. The further one penetrates into the bush the more savages one encounters. They get their food by various means. Some shoot game, others dig roots, still others raise tobacco, as well as Indian corn, or maize, which they eat raw or boiled. Besides that they trade in hides, beaver skins, and costly furs.

Those savages living close to the Europeans are frequently to be seen; some of them even understand a little English. I myself have several times seen Indian families. Once I also had the opportunity of playing the organ for a savage family at the request of Captain von Diemer. Its effect on them was that they became very merry and showed their joy and admiration by gestures and by kneeling down. Those Indians who walk about among other people only wear horse blankets instead of clothes next to their body. These are neither cut nor sewn. They wear nothing on their heads or on their feet.

Their bodies look like ours, except that they are black-yellow in color. This is not their natural color, but the Indians smear and stain themselves. Yet they are born as white as we ourselves are. Both men and women wear their hair long and smooth. The men don't like beards and when in their youth their hair begins to grow, they pull it out at once. Therefore, they have smooth faces like the women. Because of this, and because they wear the same dress, it is difficult to tell men from women. When these savages want to appear beautiful, they paint their foreheads and cheeks red, and hang their ears with strings of false beads an ell long. Under their rugs they wear neither shirts nor breeches nor skirts.

In the wilderness where they live, old and young run around naked during the summer. Every fall they come to Philadelphia in huge numbers, bringing with them various kinds of baskets which they can weave neatly and beautifully, different kinds of hides, as well as precious furs. Besides bringing these things they trade off to the governor, when they are assembled, a tract of land more than a thousand morgen in extent, and still all forest.

In the name of the province and the city they annually receive presents of many kinds, specifically blankets, rifles, rum or brandy and the like. Then they celebrate with their strange native songs, especially when they are drunk. It is impossible to understand their language. Some few of them who have had much contact with Englishmen are able to speak a little English. Among the Indians one finds some who are very strong, tall, and courageous. They "thou" and "thee" everybody in their language, even the governor himself; and they can run as fast as deer.

When one talks to them about the true and eternal God, the Creator of Heaven and Earth, they do not understand anything at all, but only answer as follows: they believe that there are two men, one good, one evil. The good man made everything that is good, and the bad man made everything that is bad. Thus it is unnecessary to worship the good man, since he is doing no one any harm. But one must pray to the bad man, so that he should do no harm to anyone. They wish to hear nothing of the Resurrection of the Dead, Salvation, Heaven or Hell. They bury their dead where they die.

Reliable people told me several times that the savages kill and bury those of their old people who are unable to move on account of age or break down on the road. But should a savage kill another human being (if it does not happen in war or on account of old age), then the murderer must die without fail, whether the dead person was one of ours or one of theirs. First they conduct the evildoer to their Indian king to be tried, thence back again to the place where the murder was committed. Then they kill him all of a sudden, bury him on the spot, and cover his grave with lots of wood and stones. On the other hand, they must receive satisfaction from us in similar cases. Otherwise they would treat an innocent white man in the same manner.

When the savages come into the city of Philadelphia and see the beautiful and marvelous buildings there, they are amazed and laugh at the Europeans for expending so much care and cost on their houses, saying: "That was quite unnecessary. After all, one could exist without such houses." They are especially amazed about European garments and finery. Indeed, they will even go so far as to spit when they see them.

When two savages get married or take their vows, then the bridegroom puts a piece of deer's leg into the bride's hand, meaning that he will nourish his future wife with meat. In return, his bride presents him with an ear of corn, to show that in future she will supply bread for her husband and children. Thus they take care of each other and remain together until death parts them.

Old savages have often been questioned about their descent and origin and have replied in this fashion: that they neither knew nor could say anything else but this — that their great-grandfathers had lived in the same wilderness, and that it was unjust of the Europeans to take their land away from them. That, however, was why they had to go further and further back into the wilderness in order to find game for their sustenance.

These savages use a remarkable weapon, a round bow. Into this they place front and center a sharp and pointed stone of a finger's length. This is a little more than an inch broad in back and as sharp as a knife on both sides. They take good aim with it; and when they hit an animal that will not fall, they run after it till they get it, for they can run faster than a horse. As evidence for this I myself brought such a stone with me, used by the Indians or savages to kill game. This was their sole weapon before they obtained guns from the Europeans.

The Reverend Mr. Schaerter or Schaertlin, who was a minister in Zell and Altbach in the Duchy of Württemberg and now serves as a preacher in Pennsylvania, in the township of Macungie in the Blue Mountains, sixty miles from Philadelphia, also made a remarkable discovery. In the year 1735, lost in the wilderness and trying to find the right way, he discovered partly buried in the ground a stone door frame on a small wooded hill. At first he thought it was natural. But when he rubbed off the moss with which it was overgrown and examined it attentively he found hewn into the upper stone and going across it, an inscription in Hebrew, reading: "Thus far the God of Joshua has helped us."

But although many foundations for the building of new houses have been laid all over this new country, and great tracts of forest and fields cleared far and wide, no sign of old habitations has been found, except by a small creek not far from Philadelphia, where there were some hewn stones laid one upon the other, which made people speculate that at this spot there must have been a building of sorts, even before the time of the savages.

In Pennsylvania everything is paid for with stamped paper money in exchange for which one may own and buy as much as one wishes. This paper money is printed in English and bears the King's seal and the governor's name. The smallest denomination is worth three kreuzer,* the second

* [At this point, the editor of the first German edition confused matters by explaining erroneously that Mittelberger had taken a kreuzer for a penny.

four kreuzer, the third six kreuzer, the fourth nine kreuzer, the fifth fifteen kreuzer, the sixth twenty kreuzer, the seventh thirty kreuzer, the eighth a half a crown, which makes forty-two kreuzer, the ninth is a whole crown, which comes to as much again, and the tenth is a twenty-shilling bill, that is, a pound, or in German money six florins. Such a piece of paper money is no bigger than a hand's breadth; and it comes in denominations of six, twelve, eighteen, and twenty-four gulden.[6] This kind of paper money may be exchanged for silver and gold. Anyone who counterfeits such officially stamped paper money is hanged without any possibility of pardon. Other than paper money, there is no other valid currency except gold in the form of French and Spanish dollars, the latter having a large circulation.

N.B. If our countrymen bring German coin into the country, they will not get a kreuzer's worth for it; that is to say, if it is small coin.

When two persons have a quarrel or lawsuit in this country and cannot settle it themselves, they must first appear before a J.P., who corresponds to a judge. When the plaintiff and witnesses prefer a charge, the J.P. asks whether they wish to persist in it, that is, whether they can swear to it. If the answer is yes, the J.P. takes the Bible in his hands, and admonishes the parties once more very sharply. At that point, they must take the Bible from the hands of the J.P. and must kiss it three times. Then the J.P. says, "Now it is done." He sits down again, binds the defendant over for the next court, and has the constable or court usher take him to prison in Philadelphia at once. There he must remain until

---

Actually Mittelberger had accurately reduced the value of the Pennsylvania currency to its German equivalents.]

[6] That is, florins, the denominations referred to being £1, £2, £3, and £4.

the next court is convened, which sometimes means waiting for almost a quarter of a year. If the defendant does not want to go to prison, he must usually deposit bail in the amount of one, two, three, four, five, or six hundred florins as a surety for his appearance and surrender at the next court in Philadelphia. If he cannot afford to do that, he must bestir himself and find a good friend to stand bail in his stead. If he does not appear at the appointed time, then the money that has been deposited, or its equivalent in property, is forfeited without fail.

When a case comes before the court for the first time, there is an immediate fee of £5, that is, 30 florins. If it is not disposed of, and is postponed until the second court, it costs as much again. And yet sometimes a case is not even settled then. But when it has been called up often enough, the gentlemen of the court choose three impartial men who are to settle the case. This happens in the following manner. When the three chosen men meet with the plaintiff and the defendant at the appointed time, two of the referees are told on whose behalf each was chosen and sworn by the court. The third man, however, who serves as the arbitrator, must make the decision if the other two cannot agree. But before the case itself is taken up, the three men, in the presence of an English clerk, prepare a bill of particulars in English, even when the affair concerns Germans. For a German document has no validity before the authorities. Both the plaintiff and the defendant must sign this bill of particulars, and must promise that both parties will abide by what the three men will set down, speak, and conclude concerning the matter. Then the case is taken up to be adjudged in favor of one or the other party.

If anyone contracts debts and is unwilling or unable to pay them at the appointed time, then he must forfeit the property he possesses. But if he owns nothing, or not enough, he must go to prison at once and must stay there until someone vouches for him or until he himself is sold into service. This happens whether he has children or not. But if he has children and wants to be released, he is frequently compelled to sell one of them into service. A person owing £5, or 30 florins, must serve a year or longer, and so in proportion to his debt. But if a child eight, ten, or twelve years old is given to settle the debt, then it must serve until the age of twenty-one.

If a man in Pennsylvania is betrothed to a woman, and does not want to be married by an ordained preacher, he may be married by a J.P. wherever he wants. It is a very common custom that the newly married, when they have plighted their troth and the pastor has blessed them, kiss each other in front of the whole congregation or the whole assembly wherever the wedding has taken place. Again, even when the banns for a couple have been read from the pulpit as often as two or three times, it is still possible for them to give each other up without incurring any costs. Even when such a couple, with their wedding guests, have already reached the church and have stepped before the altar, either of the parties who regrets the engagement is still at liberty to run away. This has happened many times. But what occurs more often is that a bride leaves bridegroom and wedding guests waiting in the church, which causes cruel laughter among the onlookers, who then partake free of charge of the wedding meal that had been prepared.

A couple who want to get married in this province despite the absolute opposition of parents and relatives on one or both sides — especially if the woman will not renounce her lover — simply ride off together on one horse. And because women have much greater privileges than men, the man must sit behind his beloved. In this position they ride to a J.P. and inform him that they had stolen one another, and ask him to marry them for a fee. When this has happened, neither parents nor friends can put any more obstacles in their way.

Those who have lost husband or wife in Germany, and have neither seen the corpse nor obtained a death certificate, are sure to find their lost treasures in America if they are still alive. For Pennsylvania is the gathering place for all runaway good-for-nothings. There one can find many wives and husbands who left their spouses and children high and dry, then got married again — only to have made a worse bargain than before.

If a man gets a woman with child and is willing to marry her, either before or after confinement, then he has atoned for his sin and is not punished by the authorities. But if he is unwilling and she sues him, he must either marry her or give her some money. Fornication as such however is not punished.

Some years ago the following incident really happened not far from the Blue Mountains. A man's wife, somewhat advanced in years, fell ill and her condition became worse from day to day. Since the woman herself lost all hope of recovery, she commended herself to God, and at the same time begged her husband not to refuse her her last request, which would be of benefit to their children. The man wanted to grant her anything he could, gave her his hand to seal the promise, and asked of what her request consisted. She replied, "Alas, my dear husband, I am much concerned about my children who are still young and immature. I am afraid that when I die they may get a bad stepmother. So I ask you most earnestly to marry no one but Rosina, who has all this time been such a faithful and hardworking servant in our house."

The husband comforted her, assuring her that she ought not to worry about the matter and expressed the hope that she would recover from her illness. She, however, had no faith in his consolation and kept on begging her husband to marry no one but Rosina, so that before she died she might know and see what kind of a mother her children would be getting.

Finally the husband had to engage to make the marriage his wife suggested — verbally and by shaking hands on it. Even this was not sufficient for her. She called Rosina to her bedside, and commended the entire household, as well as the husband and children to her care. The servant maid did not refuse, but said she would do the master's will in everything. When the anxious woman had received the assent of both parties, she made her husband and the maid join hands before her eyes, and vow that they would have and hold one another. The sick woman added her hands to theirs, blessed the new pair herself, and was delighted over the turn events had taken.

Right after this, however, the sick woman's health improved; she gained from day to day, until she finally recovered completely. At this point the husband said to his old wife, "You yourself forced me to marry the young woman, and now I intend to keep her." To which the old wife replied, "Yes, that is exactly the way I want it. Now I can die in peace when the time comes."

While the old wife was still alive, the young one gave birth to children. The old wife took good and tender care of her during her confinements; so that both wives and the husband were well content with one another. And no one made any objections, since they were not church members. After the first wife's recovery, when anyone came and asked to speak to the mistress of the house, the husband always inquired, "Which do you mean, the old or the young one?" And they themselves acknowledged that they were both his wives.

One could question the truth of my story by citing the severity of English law, which condemns to death anyone who has two wives or two husbands. But the judge does not pronounce this judgment unless one party brings suit. The two wives in my story, however, were well content. And in this instance there was another special circumstance, namely, that severe as the laws are, they cannot be strictly carried out in Pennsylvania, since people in the rural districts live too far apart from one another. As a matter of fact, if it should ever happen that the case of a man who had two wives should come before the authorities, the man would not rest easy until he had married a third wife in the bargain. For then he would go scot-free, not having transgressed against the law that forbids people to have two, but does not expressly forbid them to have three wives.

In general, however, crimes are punished severely, especially larceny. If someone steals objects of as little value as a handkerchief, a pair of stockings, shoes, or a shirt, and suit is brought against him, he is tied to a post in the public market, stripped to the waist, and lashed so terribly with a switch or even with a horse- or dog-whip in which knots have sometimes been tied that patches of skin and flesh hang down from his body. If such a one is guilty of theft once again, even if he only steals a horse or something worth twenty gulden, he receives short shrift. He is placed, bound, into a cart, transported to the gallows, and has a rope put around his neck. The cart is then driven away and he is left to hang. Many suffer miserably, and die in agony. In this country it does not matter who carries out the office of hangman; for £5, or 30 florins, anyone who wishes can do so. While I was there one of the executions had to be carried out by such a clumsy hangman (this is the name they are called). And it took him so long that finally some distinguished gentlemen who were present got impatient and called out, asking why he took so long about his business. But the hangman was a man of ready wit and answered boldly, "Gentlemen, if you can do my office better than I can, come here and perform it." At which the people laughed their fill at these gentlemen.

Everyone here is free to dispense with the services of a flayer and to take his fallen horse, cow, or whatever to any place he wishes, there to skin it himself and to do as he likes with the hide. No obstacle is placed in his way in this matter; and anyone, whatever his profession, may do it without objection.

One could travel around Pennsylvania for an entire year without spending a kreuzer. For it is the custom in this country that when a traveler comes on horseback to a house, he is asked whether he wishes to have anything to eat. Then the stranger is given a piece of cold meat, generally something left over from a meal. In addition he is given plenty of bread, butter or cheese, as well as drink. If he wants to stay overnight, he and his horse can do so, free of charge. When someone arrives at a house while a meal is in progress, he must sit down to the table at once and take pot luck. But there are also inns where one can obtain just what one wants.

Englishwomen in Pennsylvania and in all English colonies have the same qualities and privileges as do their sisters in Old England. They are exceptionally handsome and well formed, generally cheerful, friendly, very free in demeanor, plucky, smart and clever, but at the same time very haughty. They are fond of dress, and demand a great deal of attention from men. Englishmen do indeed make much of them, and respect them very highly. A man must not think of marrying a woman if he is not able to support her without her having to work. Otherwise she would make him very unhappy or even run away from him. For women must not be asked to do any work except such as they will do of their own free will.

The women are fond of receiving visits and attending parties. Whether the husband likes this or not, he must not even pull a face about it. I'd rather get into a fight with three men in England than give an Englishwoman a single slap in the face. When her own husband boxes her ears, and she complains to the neighboring women, his life is no longer safe. If it happens several times, he had better put a safe distance between himself and her; or she can see to it that he is put into prison for a long time or even sent to the galleys. And no one can force her to take her husband back. It is no wonder that Englishwomen are generally

very good-looking. They are tenderly cared for from child-
hood on, they partake of no coarse foods or beverages, they
are not allowed to work, and they spend little time in the
sun. In court the evidence of one Englishwoman is worth
that of three male witnesses. It is said that Englishwomen
received this great privilege from Queen Elizabeth.

Concerning the size of America, people in Pennsylvania
say that this part of the world is supposed to be far larger
than Europe, and that it would be impossible to explore
it completely on account of the lack of roads, and because
of the forests, and the rivers, great and small. Pennsylvania is not an island, as some simpletons in Germany believe it to be. I took the opportunity of talking about the
size of this part of the world with an English traveler, who
had been with the savages far inland. He told me that he
had been with the Indians in the country, trading for skins
and furs, more than 700 miles from Philadelphia, that is a
journey of 233 Swabian hours. He had spoken about this
topic with a very aged Indian who gave him to understand
in English that he and his brother had at one time traveled
straight across country and through the bush toward the
setting sun, starting out from the very place where the meeting with the English traveler took place. And according to
their calculation they had journeyed 1,600 English miles.
But when they realized that they had no hope of reaching
the end of the country they had turned back again.

On this trip they had encountered an indescribable number of Indians of their race, as well as many kinds of animals: white and black bears, stags (not as large as ours),
buffalo, panthers strong enough to kill cattle or men, very
large wild pigs, wolves, monkeys, foxes, and the like. Also,

feathered game of many sorts, such as golden eagles, turkeys (that is, a kind of fowl larger than a rooster), swans, wild ducks — not to mention the many marvelous birds hitherto unknown to them and especially many kinds of animals covered with very fine and valuable fur. Among others they had encountered an animal that had a smooth and pointed horn an ell and a half long and pointing straight out on its head. This animal was as big as a medium-sized horse, but could run faster than a stag. The Europeans in Pennsylvania had taken this animal for the unicorn.* The same old savage had also said that he and his brother had encountered many great bodies of water on their trip, not to mention the smaller rivers all of which they had crossed by swimming.

Various rich ores have been discovered in the Blue Mountains. But, as far as possible, these are as yet kept hidden. These ores consist for the most part of copper, sulphur, and iron, and promise a rich yield.

Several iron works or foundries and several glass works have already been built in the region. Substantial amounts of cast iron and glass are exported by ship from this province to Ireland, England, Holland, and to the other colonies. Indeed, many a vessel leaves the port of Philadelphia loaded with nothing but a cargo of iron bars.

A place, very well known to me, has also been found in Pennsylvania where there is located the most beautiful blue, white, and red marble out of which the English construct very handsome altars, pillars, and halls. These marble stones are as large as one might require them. And there are also plenty of other fine stones for construction. Freestone and

* Perhaps it is the elk.

unhewn rocks, therefore, are exclusively used in this country for building purposes.

In Pennsylvania there have already been established four printing presses: two in Philadelphia, one printing English books, one German; the third in Germantown; and the fourth in Lancaster. There are also in existence a sufficient number of flour-mills, sawmills, oil presses, fulling mills, powder and paper mills, lime and brick kilns, and tanneries and potteries. In Philadelphia there are both German and English apothecaries; in fact, I do not know of any art or trade that is not to be found in this city or in the new land. Even glaziers and scissors grinders are already making their rounds there — appearing very strange and ridiculous to the English people.

As I reported before, the only lack in this country is the cultivation of the vine; but I have no doubt that in time, this too will come.

It is no wonder, therefore, that this beautiful country, already extensively settled and inhabited by wealthy people, has excited the envy of France. Indeed, as I write, a rumor is circulating that Frenchmen invaded Pennsylvania in November 1755 and captured Lancaster, a task all the easier for them because of the disagreements between the Governor, Mr. Morris, and the Assembly. The latter did not want to appropriate any money for the defense of the country

In my humble view, Pennsylvania cannot endure a long war. There is nothing for which that country is less prepared than a war, especially because such a large number of Quakers live there who will not quarrel or fight with any one. That is why magazines or stores of grain and provisions have never been set up. Hitherto everybody in this country annually sent his surplus products for sale to Philadelphia, whence they were shipped by sea to other provinces. That is why I fully believe that if there should be a war, indescribable misery must result, from want of provisions.

Compared to Europe, Pennsylvania has a very changeable climate. During the summer it is often so hot and, so to speak, airless, that one comes close to suffocation. And wintertime is marked by frequent penetrating cold spells which come so suddenly that human beings as well as the cattle and the birds in the air are in danger of freezing to death. Fortunately these cold spells do not last long, and are interrupted by sudden changes. Often, within the space of one day, one gets three or four kinds of weather — warm, cold, stormy, rainy, snowy, and then again fine weather. Sometimes, unexpected gales and cloudbursts come, of such force that one often thinks that everything is bound to perish. Large fruit and cedar trees with their roots are sometimes ripped out of the ground, indeed often across whole tracts of forest. There are constant, violent winds in this region, because it is situated close to the open sea.

In the spring, with warm weather coming so suddenly, everything begins to grow very fast; and by the beginning of June harvesting is fully under way.

In the summer, however hot it may have been during the day, one must not remain lightly dressed after sunset, on account of the heavy and penetrating dew. Those who neglect this precaution come down at once with catarrh or even with a fever.

It is surprising to hear old Indians or savages often complain that since the Europeans came into their country they have had to suffer heavy snow, cold, and torrential rains, as well as severe and terrible thunderstorms, all of which were allegedly unknown to them before the arrival of the strangers. Whether this is true or not, even the Pennsylvanians blame the Europeans for this, because they, and especially the Germans among them, are for the most part people who use such vile and horrible oaths.

That is why a short time ago a penalty of £5, or 30 florins, was fixed upon every oath uttered in public. This penalty applies throughout Pennsylvania, to both the Germans and the English. If one person hears another swearing, and informs on him, the informer receives 15 florins, or half of the fine imposed. The consequence is that many are anxious to guard against the harm and danger that may come of this evil habit. However, the effect of this law has been to make some people avaricious for the money they can earn by informing.

During the time of my stay one of these greedy people got something he had not bargained for. When, from self-interest he informed against a very poor man for swearing, the J.P. asked him first of all whether the man who had been swearing was poor or rich, and whether he had any children. When the J.P. learned that no money could be extracted from the culprit, he ordered him given fifty lashes on his behind to make up for the fine of £5, or 30 florins. But since the informer was entitled to half of whatever exaction was made, the J.P. asked whether he would forego his share. When the informer answered this question in the negative, the justice urged him to be patient, for he would duly receive what was due him. The J.P. then ordered twenty-five good lashes to be given the accused for his profanity; after which he ordered twenty-five lashes well laid on, to be administered to the greedy informer who was not a little surprised by the turn events had taken. He who had enjoyed the misfortunes of others vowed never again to inform on anyone as long as he lived.

In the province of Pennsylvania, especially in the city of Philadelphia, the Sabbath-breakers who buy and sell on Sunday, when there is no necessity for doing so, are fined £5, or 30 florins each. Even a baker who bakes bread and sells it in his shop on Sundays or holidays is fined 30 florins. A merchant trading on Sundays has still less claim to indulgence. Grinding flour is forbidden under the same penalty. A waggoner who needlessly drives into the fields or even across the country must pay the same penalty, because driving is held to be his everyday occupation, just like any other.

Nevertheless, because of the numerous religious denominations and sects, there is great confusion. Sunday is very badly kept, especially in the rural districts, where most country folk pay little attention to it. Apostle-days and holidays are not observed at all. And, as I reported before, because the inhabitants are widely scattered and often live far from the churches, many a father holds divine service for his family in his house. Many other people plough, reap, thresh, hew or split wood, and the like. And thus Sunday is disregarded by many, especially since for want of an annual calendar many do not even know when Sundays fall. And thus the young people especially grow up like Indians or savages, without the necessary knowledge of divine things.

In Pennsylvania and the other English colonies innumerable Negroes or Blacks are forced to serve out their lives as slaves. The price of a strong and industrious half-grown Negro ranges from 200 to 300 to 450 gulden. Many are given in marriage by their masters, so that they may raise young blackamoors who are sold in their turn. These black folk are married in the English fashion.

The inhabitants of Pennsylvania may be divided into four classes, according to their color. There are:

Whites. These are Europeans who have come into the country and natives whose fathers and mothers are Europeans.

Negroes. These are Blacks brought over from Africa as slaves.

Mulattoes. These are people begotten by a white father and a black mother, or by a black father and white mother. They are neither white nor black, but yellowish in color.

The Dark-Browns. These are savages or Indians, the original inhabitants of the country.

As to the number of people in Pennsylvania, it must be confessed that the females in this new country are very fertile. For one marries young in this country, and many people arrive every year. One can come into any house in Philadelphia, or elsewhere in this country, and generally find it full of children; and the city of Philadelphia swarms with them. Whenever one meets a woman, she is either pregnant, or carries a child in her arms, or leads one by the hand Every year, then, many children are born.* Those born and brought up in this country grow very fast, and often very tall. They are full-grown at the age of fifteen, rarely later than at seventeen or eighteen.

On the other hand they seldom reach old age. In this

* There are said to be 200,000 inhabitants in Pennsylvania.

81

respect they resemble the trees in their forests. The Europeans coming into the country attain a far more advanced age than the natives born in it. I, at least, saw few natives who had lived to sixty or seventy, although I did encounter people who had arrived in this country as children with the first immigrants seventy-five years ago. These latter told me what the country looked like at that time, and how much misery they sometimes had endured.

I can well believe that the beginners in this new and savage country had a hard time of it. For this small flock had to live in a constant state of great fear, because of the Indians, or savages, swarming around them at the time. They lacked a great deal, including nearly every kind of tool. They were forced to hoe the seed into the soil because they had neither horses nor cattle. Furthermore, they were at that time and for long afterwards without flour mills, and had to crush and grind up the grain with flat stones. Bread-baking was also quite a miserable affair. To cap all this, for a long period no salt was obtainable. They had wood, and they did not lack meat since they shot all kinds of game, though there was sometimes a shortage of gunpowder. For a long time several persons had to own one horse in common, until more horses and cattle were brought in from other countries. All this apart from the multitude of wild beasts, large and small, and of snakes and vermin, which obliged them to live in great fear and worry all the time. They were also compelled to keep great fires going around their huts by day and night, to keep off bears, panthers, and wolves.

Nowadays, however, one rarely sees a bear or a panther in Pennsylvania. It is true that some years ago a big bear came by night into Captain Von Diemer's orchard, and climbed on the fruit trees from which he shook down apples as a man would, whereupon the dogs gave the alarm. The bear, however, paid no attention and kept on shaking the trees. Finally the servants reported what was happening to the master of the house who came out immediately with two rifles, his servants, and his dogs. And when by moonlight he had come close enough, he greeted the apple-shaker with a bullet. The wounded bear began to rage terribly and tumbled down from the tree wrong side up. But when the bear wanted to flee, the master fired a second shot, and after the bear had made a somersault and received a third shot, he remained lying on the ground. Then the large dogs fell upon him and strangled him. This incident filled many of the neighbors with great joy.

Old people eighty years of age also sadly told me the following about their former sorrowful condition. For a long time there had been a great lack of Godfearing preachers, and of the sacraments of Baptism and Holy Communion. And when a preacher did on occasion appear, many people had to walk ten, twenty, or thirty hours to hear him. In contrast, nowadays people would not even take an hour's walk to hear a preacher, would indeed despise him. The many sects misguide people and make many heretical. Many of our young Germans especially are easily misled; they have had to do service for so many years that they even forget their native tongue.

Many adults and old people have also changed their faith, just for the sake of their sustenance. I could quote many instances, but this would take me too far afield. I shall cite only a single example. I knew an old German neighbor of mine very well. He had been a Lutheran. Then he re-baptized himself in running water. Some time later he circumcised himself and thereafter believed only in the Old Testament. Finally, just before he died, he baptized himself again by sprinkling water over his head.

I cannot pass over yet another example of the wicked life some people lead in this free country. Two very rich planters living in the township of Oley, both well known to me, one named Arnold Hufnagel, the other Conrad Reif, were both archenemies of the clergy, scoffing at them and at the Divine Word.[7] They often met to pour ridicule and insults upon the preachers and the assembled congregation, laughing at and denying Heaven and future bliss as well as damnation in Hell. In 1753 these two scoffers met again, according to their evil habit, and began to talk of Heaven and Hell.

Arnold Hufnagel said to Conrad Reif, "Brother, how much will you give me for my place in Heaven?"

The other replied, "I'll give you just as much as you'll give me for my place in Hell."

Hufnagel spoke again, "If you will give me so and so many sheep for my place in Heaven, you may have it."

Reif replied, "I'll give them to you, if you will give me so and so many sheep for my place in Hell."

So the two scoffers struck their bargain, joking blasphemously about Heaven and Hell. When Hufnagel, who had been so ready to get rid of his place in Heaven, wanted to go down to his cellar the next day, he suddenly dropped dead. Reif, for his part, was suddenly attacked in his field by a flight of golden eagles who sought to kill him. And this

[7] Oley is a town some eleven miles south of Reading, Pennsylvania.

would have happened without fail had he not piteously cried for help, so that some neighbors came to his assistance. From that time on, he would not trust himself out of his house. He fell victim to a wasting disease and died in sin, unrepentant and unshriven. These two examples had a visible effect on other scoffers, similarly inclined. For God will not let Himself be scoffed at.

On the first and second days of May there is general merrymaking in Pennsylvania, with the principal participation by unmarried persons of both sexes. All amuse themselves with games, dancing, shooting, hunting, and the like. Those unmarried people who are native-born adorn their heads with a piece of the fur of a wild animal, together with a painting of any wild animal they choose. Thus decked out the young lads walk around the town shouting, "Hurrah, Hurrah." But only the native-born may attach such decorations to their hats; and they are called Indians.

The following custom prevails in Pennsylvania among all people, high and low, in the city as well as in the country. When one enters a house or when one encounters another person, one shakes hands first with the father and mother of the family, then, in the same manner, with all the other people, as many as there may be, sometimes as it happens with a whole roomful. Such greeting and handshaking is customary among strangers as well as among the closest friends, and the mode of address is the same with the English and Germans, "Dear good friend, how are you?" The answer is, "Fair to middling." This well-bred custom springs in part from the many English Quakers in Philadelphia, and in part from the Indians themselves, who were the first to practice it. To tell the truth, one rarely hears or sees a quarrel between the people in this country. The most distant strangers trust each other more than do acquaintances in Europe. Also, people are far more sincere and generous toward each other than in Germany. That is why our Americans live together far more quietly and peacefully than the Europeans. And all this is the result of the liberty they enjoy, which makes them all equal.

There are in this country a great many very beautiful, pearl-colored squirrels that are twice as big as ours. They are shot daily for food, because their flesh is most delicious. They are almost as long as a half-grown hare, only not quite so thick. Hares, snipe, pheasants, wild ducks, wild pigeons, and wild turkeys can also be shot in great quantity every day. Fish and fowl, too, are everywhere to be obtained in plenty. And now I recall another kind of squirrel — an exceedingly pretty flying squirrel.* This species however is very small, approximately the size of a rat, but not as thick. One can cover it with one hand. These flying squirrels can fly the distance of a rifle shot, their fur is like fine velvet, their color like that of the big squirrels, and their skins fetch a good price. I tried to bring one of these rare and wonderful creatures back with me to Germany. But during the sixth week of my ocean crossing it was unexpectedly bitten to death by a very large parrot. This parrot was bright yellow underneath, his wings were sky-blue. It was larger than a rooster and could speak a great deal of English. There were two other parrots on the ship. One was the size of a pigeon, grass green, and could speak Spanish. The third

* For a description of this flying squirrel see the German translation of M. de Dièreville's *Journey to Acadia,* p. 239.

was actually a pair — one female, one male — neither bigger than a quail, grass-green, with red heads. They could call out a great many things in English. Many kinds of such marvelous and beautiful birds are to be found in Pennsylvania.

On the other hand, it is still pretty difficult to hear good music. In the capital city of Philadelphia there is neither English nor German church music. Some Englishmen occasionally give spinet or harpsichord concerts in private houses. I brought the first organ into the country (built in Heilbronn); it now stands in a high German Lutheran Church in the city of Philadelphia. After this organ had been installed there and tuned, it was consecrated with great rejoicing, and delivered to the Christian Church of St. Michael for the praise, glory, and service of God. At this great and joyous festival there appeared fifteen Lutheran preachers as well as the entire vestries of all the Evangelical churches. The number of people present was immense. Many people came a great distance, ten, twenty, thirty, forty, up to fifty hours' journey in order to see and hear this organ. The number of people listening, standing inside and outside the church, German and English, has been estimated at several thousand. On the second day of this solemn and joyous festival all the assembled Lutheran preachers and vestries held a conference in the course of which I was appointed schoolmaster and organist. As I became better and better known in Pennsylvania, and people found out that I brought fine and good instruments with me, many English and German families came ten, twenty, up to thirty hours' journey to hear these instruments and to see the organ. And they were greatly surprised, since they had never in all their lives seen or heard an organ or any of these instruments.[8]

At the present time there are already six organs in Pennsylvania. The first in Philadelphia, the second in Germantown, the third in Providence, the fourth in New Hanover, the fifth in Tulpehocken, and the sixth in Lancaster, all of which came into the country during the four years of my stay there.

Throughout Pennsylvania both men and women dress according to the English fashion. Women do not wear hoopskirts, but everything they do wear is very fine, nice, and costly. Skirts and jackets are cut and sewn in one piece. Skirts can be parted in front. Under them women usually wear handsomely sewn petticoats trimmed with ribbon. But the outer long skirts have to reach down to the shoes, and are made of cotton, chintz, or other rich and beautiful material. All the women wear fine white aprons every day, on their shoes generally large silver buckles, round their throats fine strings of beads, in their ears costly rings with fine stones, and on their heads fine white bonnets embroidered with flowers and trimmed with lace and streamers. Their gloves are made of velvet, silk and similar kinds of material, also generally trimmed with silver or gold lace, or beautifully embroidered. Their neckerchiefs are made either of velvet or of pure silk, and are likewise richly embroidered. When the women walk or ride out, they wear blue or scarlet cloaks reaching down to the waist. On their heads they wear black or beautifully colored bonnets in-

---

[8] The consecration of the organ is also described in Henry M. Muhlenberg, *Journals* (Philadelphia, 1942), I, 276.

stead of straw hats. These bonnets are specially made and take the place of parasols, though they are prettier. If our women could see such bonnets they would at once want to have them for themselves.

When the women go riding on horseback, they use costly whips, which are elegantly made of fine wire, whalebone, and the like. The handle is usually of red velvet, of plush or tortoise shell, of ivory or mother-of-pearl, and sometimes even of solid silver, according to the price the owner is willing to pay. The women carry such whips with them when they travel in the country or go riding into town or to church. They hold on to them even in church. Many women will compete with the best male riders for a wager. An English servantwoman, especially in Philadelphia, is as well dressed as a fine lady in Germany. All Englishwomen are generally beautiful; they usually wear their hair cut short or trimmed.

The apparel of the men, especially the English, is generally very elegant and this applies to farmers as well as to the other ranks. It is all made of excellent English cloth or similar material; and the shirts are also fine. Peasants as well as gentlemen wear wigs. In Philadelphia very large and very fine beaver hats are worn; and no wonder, since Pennsylvania is the home of the beaver. But during the summer, because the heat is so great, one and all wear their hats with the rim turned down, especially in the country. For the same reason thin light coats are worn; or just a jacket neatly made of soft linen or dimity. Everyone wears long trousers that reach down to the shoes; such trousers are very wide and are made of fine stiffened linen. All the men have their hair cut quite short during summers, and wear only a cap of fine white linen and over it a hat with the rim not turned up. On entering a house they doff the hat, but not the cap. And if anyone travels even just an hour's journey over land, he wears his long coat and a pair of boots that are half turned down and reach only to the middle of the calf. One has to go dressed this way in this country, because the weather is apt to change so rapidly.

The price of farms in Pennsylvania, especially around Philadelphia, is already very high; from thirty to fifty florins must be paid for a morgen of still uncleared forest land, just a day's journey from the city. And if one wants to own a place as a homestead, in habitable and cultivated condition, containing a house, barns and good stables as well as good meadows, orchards, arable land, and sufficient woodland, then one has to pay twice as much as for uncultivated land. The price for a morgen of such land is approximately a hundred gulden. Rich Englishmen have already bought from the Indians all the remote land where everything is as yet wild and wooded, in order to sell it again at a high price to incoming Europeans. Our German people who go to this country do not even get enough free land on which to build a cottage. Furthermore, land gets more expensive every year, especially since the English know that so many people, anxious to own farms or plantations, come annually into this country.[9]

In South Carolina, 200 to 250 hours distant from Pennsylvania, one can still get a morgen for eighteen or twenty kreuzer; but it is all forest land. There one has to travel one to three hours to see one's nearest neighbor, and from two

[9] Mittelberger is somewhat harsh and inaccurate in his account of the land situation. *See* Frank R. Diffenderffer, *The German Immigration into Pennsylvania Part II The Redemptioners* (Lancaster, 1900), pp. 269–272.

to eight days to reach a town or a church. But all kinds of grain grow very well in this region. Carolina is much warmer than Pennsylvania; for it produces rice in abundance, as well as a great deal of cotton and olive oil. On the trees grow nuts as thick as a man's fist. When these fall in autumn and are opened they contain a firm ball which must be pulled apart by force and combed. After this has been done, the cotton is washed and bleached until it is white as snow. Everyone there wears cotton garments.

All houses in Pennsylvania are built solidly of hewn stone; and when they stand alone they are generally provided on every side with large English plate glass windows. One rarely sees stoves in their rooms. Instead, all the houses have French fireplaces. One and all sit in front of them, drinking their good English beer or the like, and smoking their pipefuls of tobacco. When these fireplaces are well built, no smoke escapes into the rooms.

All houses have two benches on each side, set up about four feet straight out in front of the doors. Resting on two columns over each bench is a roof like that of a garden pavilion. These benches are to be found not only in the country, but also in front of all the houses in Philadelphia. Every evening when the weather is fine people sit on the benches, or promenade in front of them. The streets and houses of this city are so straight that one can look directly ahead for the distance of a half hour's walk.

There are seven principal churches in the city, as mentioned previously. But only one has a steeple. This, however, is beautifully constructed and very tall. In the entire city there are two small bells; and when they are rung together, it means that it is time for all church services to begin. However, during the last year of my stay there, the city council and all the church vestries arranged for three bells of various sizes to be brought over from London in Old England. In the rural districts no church has a steeple, nor is any provided with a bell or clock. And so the whole year long one hears neither ringing nor striking of bells. This makes it very dull for newcomers, especially at night, until they get used to it. But almost everyone, farmers as well as gentlemen, uses a silver pocket watch; these are generally worn even by Englishwomen.

In 1754 some French deserters, according to their own report, met with a strange misfortune. Two of them came to Philadelphia and related the following adventures. Seven of their number had deserted from their regiment, then stationed beyond the great river Ohio, with the intention of taking refuge in Carolina. They had gone completely astray in the wilderness, had wandered over hill and dale, and had not encountered anyone except occasional savages. And so they strayed about for four whole weeks. After they lost sight of the Indians and had run out of food, they had subsisted for a time on venison, as long as their powder held out. After that was all gone, they came across some large rattlesnakes from which, at first, they ran away in terror. But, suffering intensely from hunger, they recalled that the savages were in the habit of eating these reptiles. So they killed some of them and ate their flesh after roasting it on the fire for a while. The meat proved harmless and in no way poisonous. At length, when they had finished this, and there was no more, they did not know where to turn next.

After long marches by day and by night through many forests and swamps, crossing rivers large and small, they became so exhausted and feeble that they could barely continue to walk, and were fully convinced that that they were doomed to collapse and perish of hunger. They then agreed to cast lots to determine which of their number was to die first. They would kill him and consume his flesh. Their corporal gave them this advice, and they all assented to it. The first lot fell upon the corporal himself. Shocked by the outcome, he did not resist and said, "I would starve to death anyway, and all of you are bound to meet the same fate." They tied him up at once, killed him, roasted him, and began to eat his flesh. This sustained them for awhile, and they were able to march on. When hunger began to press hard on them once more, they threw lots again, and continued this procedure until only two were left of the original seven. As this point these two met some people, remained alive, and at last reached Philadelphia. This sad and lengthy journey lasted from the beginning of May until the end of June.

There is a saying current in Pennsylvania to the effect that it is a paradise for women, a purgatory for men, and a hell for horses.

On September 21, 1753, the new calendar was introduced in Pennsylvania and in all the English colonies in America. Accordingly one jumped all at once from the eleventh to the twenty-first of September. This innovation met with a great deal of opposition from High Church people as well as from the sects. To some especially it was a great grievance that one Sunday and its entire Gospel lesson was to be omitted and thus entirely lost.*

With regard to the climate in Pennsylvania, it must be

---

* A strange grievance, which, to be consistent, one would have in most years; since the Gospel lessons on the twenty-fifth, twenty-sixth, and twenty-seventh Sunday after Trinity are often lost in exactly the same way.

observed that the Summer and Winter seasons differ from those in Europe; the days and nights are about three hours shorter or longer than with us. In summer, when the days are longest, about St. John's Day, the day does not begin until 4:30 A.M. and it is completely dark by 8 o'clock in the evening. On the other hand, in wintertime, when the days are shortest, they are longer here and the nights shorter than in Europe. For by 5:30 A.M. it is fully day, and night does not set in until 6:00 P.M. It is also noteworthy that when the sun has set in America in the evening, it is completely dark in half or a quarter of an hour; whereas at home it is still light for a good half hour. It is also to be remarked that when the sun has risen in Europe, America still gets three hours of night; whereas when the sun has set in Europe, America still gets three hours of sunshine. Thus Pennsylvania must be very far away from us. I have often heard captains and sailors say that according to their reckoning the distance across the sea alone, from land to land, is 3,600 miles, or 1,200 German hours. As to the depth of the sea, they informed me that when one is at a distance of one hundred miles from land, the bottom of the sea can not be fathomed, even by sinking a sounding lead at the end of a rope 50,000 fathoms long [sic!] into the sea — something that has often been tried.

In the province of Pennsylvania three principal roads have been constructed, all of which lead from Philadelphia into the country as far as it is inhabited. The first runs from Philadelphia to the right hand by the Delaware to New Frankfort; the second or middle road runs toward Germantown, Reading,[10] and Tulpehocken, extending across the

[10] Rittingston in the German original referred either to Reading or to

Blue Mountains; the third road runs to the left toward Lancaster and Bethlehem, where there is a monastery and convent full of Dunker Brethren and Sisters. The men do not shave their beards; many among them have beards half an ell in length. They wear cowls like the Capuchin monks, in winter of the same cloth or at least the same color, in summer, however, of fine white linen. The Sisters dress in the same manner. These people are not baptized until they are grown up and can testify to their faith, when it is done by dunking in deep water. They keep Saturdays instead of Sundays as holidays. Their convent Sisters, however, frequently bring forth living fruit with much patience.[11]

Redding Furnace. *See* Theodore W. Bean, ed., *History of Montgomery County Pennsylvania* (Philadelphia, 1884), p. 565.
[11] Luke 8:15.

III
THE RETURN TO GERMANY

III

THE RETURN TO GERMANY

IN conclusion I just want to relate how on my voyage home, when sea and wind were still, I saw various kinds and sizes of fish without number. Among them and especially to be noted are the large sharks or man-eaters, of which very often whole schools could be seen floating on the surface of the sea. They have the same shape as hogs, but are as large as oxen, and blow up water to the height of a man. Many of these sharks came within a stone's throw of the ship. Sometimes they set up a tremendous roar which always portended that a great storm was coming up.*

In 1750, while I was on my way to America, a large shark was caught and taken on board another ship by means of a hook to which a piece of meat was attached. And when the shark was opened up, there was found in its bowels the body of a man, completely intact. He still had on shoes with silver buckles; and this led to the surmise that this man had not died a natural death, for in that case one would not have dropped him into the water with his shoes and buckles on. Rather, he must have fallen overboard from carelessness, as happens to many people during storms. At sea, when the weather was calm, I often saw many flying fish that could fly for as long as they were wet. The largest are often about

---

* This seems to be none other than the fish *canis carcharias,* called Hayfish by the Dutch, and for which almost every nation has a different name. Shark appears to be its English name.

a foot in length, and have long fins that look like wings. They are pursued and devoured by other fish. The fish caught by us at sea always supplied fresh and welcome food. They were of different beautiful colors, some sky-blue with yellow marks, others golden-yellow with red marks, still others white with blue stars. All these fish were generally from four to six feet in length.

On our way home across the sea we experienced two dangerous and terrible gales. The first came right at the beginning, early on a Sunday morning. While it lasted the sailors had to furl up the sails. But the wind blew so violently into the sails that the middle one could not be budged even by twelve men, and the second mate had to climb up the mainmast. Even this did not help. The storm finally tore the sail out of the hands of the sailors and knocked the second mate down, so that he fell dead on the ship's deck. The storm raged for over twenty-four hours; the sea rose so high that the waves rolled over each other like great mountains, and fell roaring into the ship; so that the man at the helm and the two sailors manning the pump had to be tied fast lest they should be washed overboard by the waves. At that time we gave ourselves as well as the ship up for lost.

During the seventh week, on September 22, we had another gale so terrible and powerful that the sailors were unable to furl up all the sails. The wind blew so violently that it tore one of the biggest sails into shreds, though it had been tied fast with strong, thick rope. The waves of the sea were incredibly big; so that the ship now rode their crests, then in their troughs, and was tossed from side to side. All the time the waves rolled over the ship, so that everyone thought that the vessel was bound to sink and the people in it to perish. This gale and the terrible fear that came with it lasted from four o'clock in the evening until about three o'clock of the second night, at which point the wind subsided. But the sea and the waves were still so powerful that same day, and so wild and high, that the ship rocked and rolled violently and it was impossible to eat or cook, or in fact, to do anything at all. The poultry on board ship was for the most part found dead afterwards; the sheep and the pigs were sick, and so the crew itself very nearly perished.

When the captain's calculations showed that the journey's end was approaching he called his mates together on the last day of the eighth week and he ordered them to furl up all the sails and, when this was done, to throw out the sounding lead in order to see if it touched bottom. When all this had been done, bottom was found to be seventy-two fathoms deep, which was joyous news for us passengers because we hoped to see land soon; which indeed we did in short order. On the fourth day of the ninth week we came close to the headland of Old England. This headland looks white as snow and is therefore known as the chalk hills. But as we approached land, and had turned a large corner of France on our right, we struck a sandbank that threatened to strand and sink the ship. Fortunately the tide was just beginning to come in, and a good strong wind came up, which buoyed up the ship, and, praise be to God, led us safely out of our tribulation.

Thus, after nine weeks, and after suffering many discomforts, perils, and mortal dangers, we entered the Thames on October 10, 1754, and landed safely on the same day on which four years before I had stepped on American soil. Then we all thanked God from the bottom of our hearts;

and I kissed the ground for joy, and indeed took to heart the one hundred and seventh Psalm, which describes so well the anguish of those who go down to the sea.

To God in Three Persons for this great
mercy and preservation be praise and
thanksgiving rendered now and
forevermore.

THE JOHN HARVARD LIBRARY

*The intent of
Waldron Phoenix Belknap, Jr.,
as expressed in an early will, was for
Harvard College to use the income from a
permanent trust fund he set up, for "editing and
publishing rare, inaccessible, or hitherto unpublished
source material of interest in connection with the
history, literature, art (including minor and useful
art), commerce, customs, and manners or way of
life of the Colonial and Federal Periods of the United
States . . . In all cases the emphasis shall be on the
presentation of the basic material." A later testament
broadened this statement, but Mr. Belknap's inter-
ests remained constant until his death.*

*In linking the name of the first benefactor of
Harvard College with the purpose of this later,
generous-minded believer in American culture the
John Harvard Library seeks to emphasize the importance of Mr. Belknap's purpose. The John Harvard
Library of the Belknap Press of Harvard University
Press exists to make books and documents
about the American past more readily
available to scholars and the
general reader.*

Date Due

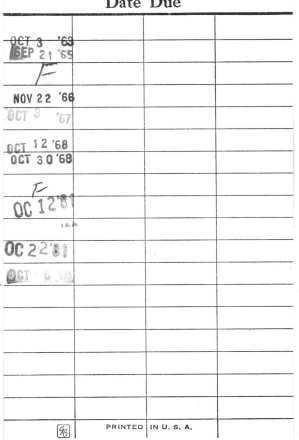

OCT 3 '63			
SEP 21 '65			
NOV 22 '66			
OCT 3 '67			
OCT 12 '68			
OCT 30 '68			
OC 12'81			
OC 22'81			
OCT 6			
	PRINTED	IN U. S. A.	

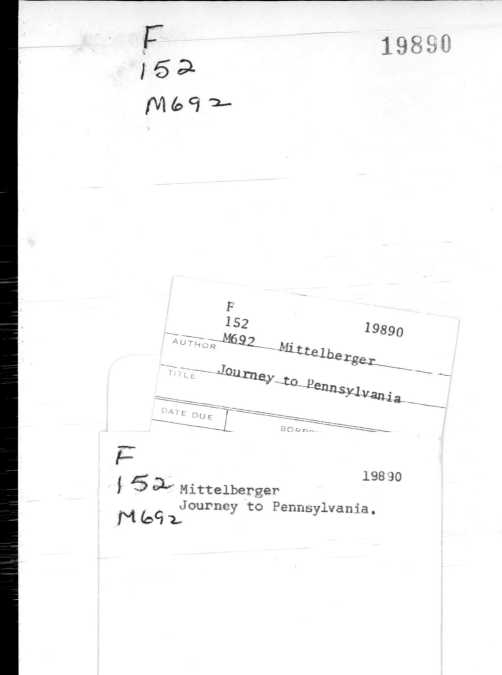

Burnets Hügel Collis

Hier sind lauter Berge die man nicht passieren kan.

Montes inaccessi

Wÿoming

Pars orientalis

Mineral Quell fons mineral

Broadhead

B U C K S

Gnadenhütten

Lizareth

Bethlehem

Der Ost-Arm von Susquehanna Fluss.

Schamokin

Fichtenwald Sylva pinorum

Truckers Co

Croushall

Durham

Lecheia

Moxunay

St. Anton Wildniss Desertum orientale

oder der Kittatinny-Berg sive Kittatinni

ga coerulea

Swatara Creek

Maiden Saucona

Tulpehoccan Cr.

Moselm Mill Crek

Hau Cock

Jacobi Cr.

Wrights

Neshaminy

laue Gebürge

Rey Hügel Monacazi

Swamp Cr. Scepack

Northwales

Wasserfall

Tone hwaqa

Sikselon Cr.

Weisers

Reading

Warwich

Reding

Schuylkill Fluss

Plymouth

German Town

Frank

Ephraim

Conventri

Pickering

Memgn Haverford

Schuppenburg

Lancaster

Great

tonalte ga

Ways

Millcor

Die Diffaum Mäuer

Neus

PHILADELPHIA

Derby

L A N C A S T E R C O M I T

E

Mall Creek

Rock

Pigeonhalls

Pigeonhalls

Cresop Susqu harini

York

Mill Cr.

Pequa

Octorara Co.

C H E S T E R C O M

Goshen The Cap Redilay Sop

Wilminton

Chester Co.

Codoras Creek

Muddy Run

Susquehanna Flun.

Elck Woottingham

Christen Cr.

Neu Castle

Oldmans

Salem

Redi I.

Allewas Cr.

Tieffer Fluss

Monacacy Creek

Halls

Charles Ins.

St. Georg

Bohemia George Town Salsefras Run

Nocentown

N E U C A S T L E

Ioppa

Neu T.

Neu Town

Chester Run.

Salisburi

D E L A W A R E

Little Cr.

D E L A W A R E S I N

Gre

Ford

Berg Spitzen

Magotti R.

Kent Insula

Dover

Mother

Milsdon Cr.

Brune hok

Potomack Flun.

Annapolis

M A R Y L A N D

C H E S E P E A C K I N

D E L A W A R E C O M I T.

S U S S E X C O M.

Cedar Cr.

Broad Cr.

Goose Cr.

V I R G

Mile Creek Hunting Cr.

London T.